London
Architecture
Biennale 2006
Change

London Architecture Biennale 2006

Change

Published by August | Cultureshock in collaboration with LAB06

First published by AugustProjects
and Cultureshock Media in
collaboration with the London
Architecture Biennale 2006

AugustProjects
Studio 6, 2–4 Hoxton Square,
London N1 6NU, UK

Cultureshock Media
27B Tradescant Road,
London SW8 1XD
Editorial Director: David Redhead
Publishing Director: Phil Allison
Editors: Tom Phongsathorn
and Kate Jazwinski
Researcher and Editorial: Emily Dixon
Copy Editor: Ian Massey
Production Manager: Nicola Vanstone

Design: Matt Brown, Stephen Coates
and Simon Esterson

Published to coincide with the
London Architecture Biennale,
16-25 June 2006
Director: Peter Murray, Wordsearch
Deputy Director: Stella Buchan-Ioannou
Treasurer: Richard Jones, Jackson Coles
Sponsorship Co-ordinator: Ann Shuptrine
Team Assistant: Natalie Creary
Team Assistant: Amanda Barry
Design and Research: Shakeeb Abu
Hamdan

ISBN: 1-902854-25-x

Printed by Graphicom, Italy
Repro: DawkinsColour, London
and Threesome Design

Distributed by Cornerhouse
Tel: +44(0)161 200 1503
www.cornerhouse.org/books

This catalogue was made possible with
the generous support of Allford Hall
Monaghan Morris, Building Design
Partnership and the Biennale Director
Peter Murray

ALLFORD HALL MONAGHAN MORRIS

Contents

The rise and rise of architecture

Foreword by Peter Murray

It was some 23 years ago that, with a like-minded group of people, I started *Blueprint* magazine with the aim of widening the architectural debate. We believed passionately that if the general quality of design in the environment was to improve, an understanding of architecture must be imbedded in our national culture. The magazine achieved a certain success at the time within a fairly limited group (and has since gone on to greater things), but it was a group that included journalists, broadcasters and opinion formers who began to write more about architecture, to produce programmes about it and to discuss issues openly and more widely.

As I contemplate the start of the second London Architecture Biennale I am convinced that we have come a long way from the time when architecture was just something that people complained about. The first LAB in 2004, which was held in Clerkenwell because it has more architects per square metre than anywhere in the world, was organised as a little local event, but its popularity took us quite by surprise. In 2006 we have been encouraged by a huge groundswell of response from the architecture and design community – including the schools of architecture – to prepare exhibitions, events, publications and installations.

There is an enthusiasm too from the general community, from businesses and from local authorities who are excited about the potential of architecture and planning and its ability to change and improve the lives of people using the city.

With this growth comes a lot of work and an insatiable thirst for funds. I would like to thank those who have given the biennale such great support – our sponsors and our partners; the members of the 250 Club (who each donated £250); Peter Ackroyd, our president, whose writings on London have greatly increased our understanding of this complex metropolis; our committee; deputy director Stella Buchan-Ioannou, without whom it just wouldn't have happened; our treasurer Richard Jones, without whom we would all be broke; and the rest of the hard-working team who co-ordinated all the events.

Some of the like-minded group of people mentioned above have also contributed to the biennale and this catalogue – I am grateful to them too. I see the meteoric growth of the biennale as a sign that those early struggles were worthwhile and helped to shift the cultural consciousness of the capital.

Peter Murray is director of the London Architecture Biennale

The soul of a city
Peter Ackroyd

This biennale is in the broadest possible sense a celebration of London itself, with the emphasis upon its material being – upon its texture and its fabric. But there is also a spiritual London to which we can turn during the festival, a city that Blake venerated as "Infinite London".

The buildings rise and fall, but the place remains for ever. The site, the soil, is the *genius loci*. It is my belief that the territorial imperative of London is as strong as ever; it is a localised force that actively affects or changes the destinies and perceptions of the people who live in this place. It is the force that drives us onward. It is the force that creates those multiple networks of fate and coincidence that are part of London's adventure. It is the spirit that dominates areas such as Clerkenwell or Southwark. It is the haunting presence of Newgate in the streets of that vicinity. It is the elusive ghost of the ancient City in the narrow streets of the present City of London. It is the tribal memory of the old sacred river in the contemplation of the present Thames.

There are parts of London that have always been the site of tears. There are neighbourhoods that have for hundreds of years been marked by sexual licence. There are those where new developments do not "stick". Kingsway and New Oxford Street, for example, are still anonymous because they were driven roughshod over streets and dwellings that had endured for many centuries. They will never be accepted. They will never be "home", as Drury Lane or Borough High Street have become home.

So we should learn to celebrate the inner life of London, expressed through its buildings, shining through its vast and intricate topography, but still somehow deeper and darker than these manifestations of its present life.

Peter Ackroyd is president of the London Architecture Biennale and a novelist, biographer and poet. His history of the city, London: The Biography *(2000), has been acclaimed as a modern classic. For this year's festival he has teamed up with Bisset Adams, Wordsalad, Foster and Partners and engineers Arup to use the Millennium Bridge as a site for an exhibition about the River Thames*

Tom Dyckhoff

London: a mad mother of invention

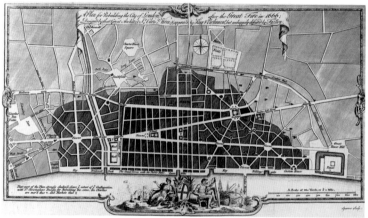

"A brilliant wind-swept, sunny day, with the fountains like hay-cocks of prismatic glitter in the shadow of Nelson's Column, with the paving stones almost opalescent, with colour everywhere. Is that 'London'? Or is it the chaotic crowd, like of baggage wagons huddled together after a great defeat, blocked in the narrow ways of the City, an apparently indissoluble muddle of grey wheel traffic, of hooded carts, or 'buses drawing out of line, of sticky mud, with a pallid church wavering into invisibility towards the steeple in the weeping sky, or grimy upper windows through which appear white faces seen from one's level on a 'bus-top. Is this again 'London'?" Ford Madox Ford, *The Soul of London*

If, during the Creation, God had inadvertently invented London, maybe sometime after finishing off the firmament and every living creature that moveth, he'd have chucked it in the bin, pronto. It wouldn't have got past the first sketch. Who would have come up with such madness? Just look at it. Can you imagine the elevator pitch for the Finchley Road? No, London has always been the city of chaos, a vulgar, cruel city. And that's exactly how we like it.

Here the merchant is king – not the monarch, not the aristocrat. London is a marketplace first – whether it's Saxons selling oysters on Fish Street or yuppy geezers shifting futures in Broadgate – and a city second. Always "business before beauty", notes Roy Porter in *A Social History of London*. We don't have Paris's *liberté, egalité* and *fraternité*. Here the common spirit is individualism, the city a mass of accumulated small actions – generally about generating filthy lucre. In London anything goes, so long as you're making money. Infringe that right and a world of trouble falls on your head.

Try, though, to do anything for the common good, a sewer perhaps, or an uncracked pavement, and you have to crawl through red tape that'd make Byzantium seem a doddle.

Adapting to chaos
Those who survive the chaos moan about the city, but make do in the muddle. We adapt to it and adapt it. Look closely and London's chaos is, in fact, a minutely organised chaos, like a coral reef or an Amazonian rainforest. We've had no powerful unified, unifying government since the Romans, whose thoroughly logical and no doubt perfectly functioning grid-iron city (I bet they'd never suffer the Circle Line) was soon abandoned for the thoroughly illogical place we live in today,

Above: Buckingham Palace, designed by Achille Louis Martinet in 1862. Above right: John Nash's design for the bottom of Regent Street. Right: with his 1931 tube diagram, Harry Beck rationalised the chaos out of the map of London

Overleaf: congestion Edwardian style. A traffic jam in front of London's Royal Exchange at Bank in the early years of the twentieth century

governed in fragments: boroughs, wards, parishes, guilds, mayors, Lord Mayors, LCCs, GLCs, GLAs. It remains an essentially medieval city – just as Paris is an Enlightenment one – ruled over by customs subject to no rational rules.

It may not work well, but it's our city, a fact despised by those, such as King John or Margaret Thatcher, who try to snatch away our muddled independence. Though any uppity so-and-so who tries to rule or organise the capital, especially archbishops, kings and town planners, are either ritually humiliated, or, well, beheaded. Compared with Charles I, Ken Livingstone gets off lightly with the mere scorn of taxi drivers and the *Evening Standard*. London is, after all, the city of debunkers of authority, of satirists and cynics, of Hogarth, Dickens and Craig Brown, mocking yet secretly revelling in the muck.

No, we have no Peter the Great, no Baron Haussmann. Our *grands projets*, such as Wren's or John Evelyn's plan to magisterially rebuild the city after the Great Fire, rarely leave the drawing board. Instead, we scorn such pompous folly. London's default setting is one of chaos, selfishness, grime. The dingy alley I live in, its puke-coloured (occasionally literally), cheap London stock bricks caked in pigeon crap, rubbish accruing with scant

prospect of being collected, always seems somehow more London than any number of regimented Belgravian terraces. Not that I wouldn't be averse to a Belgravian terrace. Or at least the rubbish being collected.

This chaos both frees you and traps you. It's why so many come, and why so many try to leave, though attempting to escape London, especially via that Finchley Road of a Friday night, is always like pulling your legs from quicksand. London is the archetype of the uncontrollable, sometimes darkly chaotic, anarchic, nihilistic city, the model for Los Angeles or Mexico City, impossible to understand in its entirety, especially by a fresh-faced greenhorn newly arrived, plop, in its soupy suburbs. There are few, treasured spots such as Primrose Hill, Parliament Hill, Gipsy Hill, where you can lift your head above the jungle canopy, and few representations, such as Harry Beck's cunning Underground map, to bring it under mental control. The only way to encapsulate it, as recent chroniclers such as Iain Sinclair and Peter Ackroyd have discovered, is through the journey, the episode, the process, the impression.

Back from the brink again
This glorious chaos periodically brings the city to the point of collapse. London is continually being declared

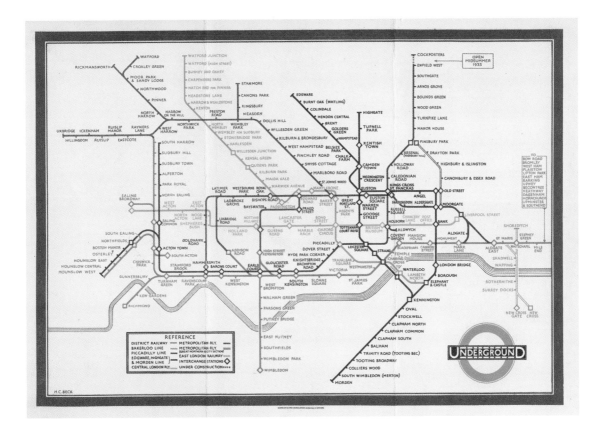

clapped out, ruined. And sometimes it is. Sometimes it rallies against destruction from beyond and within – Boudicca, say, the Great Fire, or the Blitz. But sometimes it implodes, its rickety infrastructure collapsing, falling in on its own crap. Sometimes, as in the case of plague and cholera, or the 1854 Great Stink, almost literally. Collapse can happen in boom times, the metropolis growing through amassed individual actions without the communal structure required to support it. (London's first native chronicler, John Stow, was appalled at the state of the city after its first heyday, the Elizabethan age. In *The Survey of London* he bemoaned the city's overcrowding, and the swollen sprawl beyond its walls, like a sixteenth-century Simon Jenkins: "Both sides of the streete bee pestered with buildings, with Cottages, and Allies, even up to White chapel church; and almost halfe a myle beyond it.") But collapse more often occurs when the capital is on its uppers. Post-war deindustrialisation hit London worse than most because it was the pre-eminent city of the world; the city of empire. The harder they come. In the 1980s the Thatcher government tried, superficially at least, to appeal to its entrepreneurial spirit. But the sheer size of the project means it's taken until today for London to dust itself down.

The dinginess of the 1980s did encourage much of the creative vibrancy that the city's current success is built on: its decrepit old inner-city, for instance, became inspiration and home for its new breed of satirists, the Brit Artists. But this was a moment when what London really needed was not the free market, not its government being abolished, but a jolly good bit of old-fashioned sorting out.

The impulse to improve
That was the case in Hogarth's London when, aghast at the city's shabby face as Britain was rising to empire, and perhaps cheesed off by the bloody traffic jams on The Strand, aristocrats, allied with the new breed of gentlemen architects, set about beautifying and, as they called it, "improving" the city. Often it was for the private good of their own class. Sometimes, though, solving individual inconvenience required everyone, all classes, to pull together in one of the capital's rare moments of cohesion, to build new roads, bridges, hospitals, sewers, embankments. And the best combination of all was to do this while turning a profit: hence two of London's great gifts to the world – the property speculator and his creation, the Georgian square. True, the Georgians' individual contributions were nothing to match the

Right: poll tax riots
in Trafalgar Square,
April 1990.

grandeur of Paris – how architecturally weak are the National Gallery and Buckingham Palace? – but *en masse* Georgian London formed the perfect stage set for its Victorian moment of glory. The city probably never looked more stunning.

Architects, developers and politicians are forever sorting London out, unpicking its mess, unclogging its arteries and battling with its NIMBYs to make it a little less maddening to live in. The 2012 Olympics, and the somehow inevitably chaotic Thames Gateway, are prompting the city to embark on one of those reforming moments right now. But so many, like the Georgians, misunderstand London's *raison d'etre*: the Prince of Wales, perhaps, who in his 1988 *A Vision of Britain* looked upon its unruly, gap-toothed post-war skyline and wished, how he wished, it were Venice.

Reform without revolution

But London has very rarely been beautiful. Instead, it's like a loveable, clapped-out old banger. All you can really do is ride it, and perhaps influence its course. The skill is in diagnosing its ailment as precisely as a surgeon, not going at it with a machete. If it conks out, you patch it up, tinker with the engine, give it a polish. The engine purrs and we're cruising.

Perhaps that's why it has never erupted into revolution, as Marx so often complained. We can't be arsed. We know that nothing's going to shift this city *en masse*; nothing's going to get us from Camden Town to Camberwell in under 90 minutes. But we do know that tinkering, the good old British bodge, the cunning invention, might get the old beauty purring. It is a city of permanent reform, never revolution. Necessity is the mother of invention, and London has always been, will always be, a very needy city. But its inhabitants are damn cunning inventors, who have evolved and adapted with their city, and adapted it with inventions sometimes bonkers, inventions that couldn't have happened any other place – the bollard, perhaps, that doubles as a ventilation shaft on Gracechurch Street, the railway that drives trains by vacuum, a shoulder-height bench to help Victorian porters to rest their back-breaking load for a moment, the Necropolis railway, the doubledecker bus – but which occasionally, very occasionally, change the world, as well as this mad, glorious metropolis.

Tom Dyckhoff is architecture critic of The Times and curator of the 'Big London Brainstorm' an exhibition of inventions to make the city a little nicer at the biennale hub, Smithfield House, 16-25 June

London's five great gifts to the world's cities
Tom Dyckhoff

Above: Wilhelm Trübner's turn of the century painting of Ludgate Hill captured the buzz of the city once known as "The Smoke"

The property developer
Who else but a Londoner could have come up with property speculation, the pretence of beautifying the city hiding a damn good way to make a fortune by constantly reinventing the same patch of land time and again? Stuart kings wanted London for themselves, but were no match for the rabidly ambitious property developers that came in the wake of the Great Fire; developers both aristocratic, such as the Earl of Bedford, and ordinary, such as Nicholas Barbon and William Newton. They generated that enduring myth of the capitalist city, its streets paved with gold: you too can make it here. Or you could end up ruined in a poky bedsit in Norwood.

The suburb
You've got to admire John Nash. Regent Street, Regent's Park, Buckingham Palace, Trafalgar Square – all his, the last glorious gasp of the Georgian plan to dress the capital in glorious clothes more fitting for its rising role on the world stage. But Nash's most influential work was almost an afterthought – Park Village, a picturesque collection of villas in eclectic styles, built as an experiment beside Regent's Park. Londoners, and the rest of the world, snapped them up.

The underground railway
Sometimes the whole of London needs a good sorting out. That time was 1843, and the man to do it was John Pearson. The capital's population had doubled in 40 years, and you should have *seen* the traffic on Ludgate Hill. Pearson's idea? An underground railway to link the new mainline stations, from Paddington to Farringdon, and goad people into leaving the overcrowded, slum-ridden city centre. Twenty years of mockery and slog later it opened, alas six months after Pearson died.

The terraced house and square
The finest invention of the property developer was "conditioned from the first", writes architectural historian John Summerson, "by the economic need to get as many houses as possible on to one street". And yet what variety can be wrenched from such a simple formula of two rooms, a corridor and a patch of land out back?

The work of Cedric Price
The late Cedric Price was a satirist, a socialist and a romantic. He both diagnosed London's ills and came up with solutions, perfectly in tune with its spirit of energetic anarchy, and perfectly predicting its future role as a world city of spectacle. His plans for the GLC to revive the South Bank in the mid-1980s included a giant Ferris wheel for us to gawp at "cow-pat London": familiar? My favourites, though, were his Magnets, subversive temporary devices across London, like Trojan horses – arcades, piers, bridges – for people to discover their city anew. "Architecture must be a facilitator of delight," he said. "It must make you say WOW." If only he were still alive: he'd get the Olympics sorted.

Robert Maxwell

A very British biennale

Left: Borough
Market engraved by
Gustave Doré in 1872

Above and right:
St Bartholomew
Fair, revived on its
Smithfield site for
the London
Architecture
Biennale

The idea of a biennale, like the word itself, is Italian. The first was organised in Venice in 1895, and was a celebration of the decorative arts. After the First World War innovative art came to the fore, and the biennale began to advance the tradition of modernity, while modernity itself was still happening. This drew the attention of the fascist government, which in 1930 took over the organisation from the Venice City Council. Nevertheless, it did not, or could not, stop the development of new ideas, the starting up of a music festival (1930), an international film festival (1932), a theatre festival (1934). That led on to the offering of grand prizes in the art section, and the Venice Biennale took on most of the pizzazz that it has today.

After the war it was boosted by securing the interest of Carlo Scarpa, who between 1948 and 1972 carried out a series of remarkable interventions, a circumstance that undoubtedly enhanced the attraction of the show for architects, already drawn to Venice for its architecture. This success has continued in more recent times, with the introduction of new prizes such as the Golden Lions. I was present in 1980 when Aldo Rossi, in dispute over some question of precedence, hurled his Golden Lion to the ground in disgust. Being made of plaster, it shattered – to the

great enjoyment of the crowd. The atmosphere was somewhere between a fashion show and a volcanic eruption. Venice as a background made you feel you were on holiday, and the presence of celebrities made you feel it was the only place to be.

The idea of festival has achieved even greater success, with heavies such as the Bayreuth Festival or the Festival of Aix-en-Provence drawing huge numbers every summer. In a way, the festival has come into being to exploit tourists, tourism being one of the world's top industries, something that derives more from place than it does from industrial know-how. Today, we all want to visit everywhere in our longing to be part of a global family, and we are all part of the tourist industry, both as hosts and as visitors.

In music, the ideal is the out-of-doors concert, where the glow of a summer evening adds to the dreams induced by the music. Cyril Connolly wrote a book called *Ideas and Places*, and the association of place and occasion probably encloses the human idea of happiness. As with weddings and funerals. As with memorable meals. When a place acts as host to a festival, the setting brings a unique source of memory and enjoyment. So, no wonder that Peter Murray has invented the London Architecture Biennale, now in its second manifestation,

as a way of inculcating enjoyment of place and occasion.

This year the setting is a route that goes from the British Library in Euston Road, through Percy Circus to Clerkenwell by way of Exmouth Market, around Smithfield Market past St Bartholomew's Hospital, then across the Millennium Bridge from St Paul's, past Shakespeare's Globe to Southwark Cathedral and Borough Market, with a branch to the new Architecture Foundation site (Zaha) and Tate Modern. It thus draws together both sides of the river, emphasising the way that London has regenerated the Thames as its focus and *raison d'etre*. Events and shows during the biennale will take place along this route, making it into a 5km long exhibition with the surrounding city as the subject.

The connection to markets is not accidental – Peter has a lively appreciation of the market, both as a source of commerce and a traditional way of joining place and occasion. He also clearly enjoys the benefits of opening the city to the more sophisticated mammals: remember those cows grazing in St John's Street? This year the opening of the biennale will be marked by a herd of sheep being driven across the Wobbly Bridge by a genuine shepherd with the unlikely help of Lord Foster. The fact that London still has street markets, perpetuating an ancient tradition, proves that

it is neither simply a factory nor workplace, but a centre of life. The traditional fair at St Bartholomew's will be re-created as a unique event, as a focus of celebration.

The first biennale lasted for ten days, attracted 25,000 people and raised almost £7,000 for charity. This was a real achievement. We can expect the second to go further and do more. There will also be a National Architecture Student Festival, when students will work with local school children to design and build interventions along the route. The biennale begins with a "sermon" by Renzo Piano in Southwark Cathedral.

Walking tours, bike tours, meals with key speakers, debates, talks, film shows, concerts, exhibitions, installations and a charity auction will ensure that not a moment is lost. There will be an Architecture, Art and Design show in the British Library piazza. The event that I particularly look forward to is the passeggiata, a promenade along the biennale route, starting in Borough Market with breakfast, then a meaty lunch in Smithfield's Grand Avenue, coffee and gelato in St John's Square, drinks in Exmouth Market and sundown drinks at St Chad's in King's Cross. One would like to see whole families engaging in this event, as I saw occurring in Salerno recently, when the crowd proceeded both clockwise and anti-

Left: the country
comes to London.
Two bullocks and a
herd of sheep cross
Waterloo Bridge in
1939. Below: one of
the balloons that
mark the 2006
biennale route

clockwise at once, going first by the sea front, then by
Main Street one block back. The continuing vitality of
the Italian tradition of the passeggiata is proof that cities
can be won back from being mere traffic networks, and
can offer a regenerated urban space as a setting for
human events.

Architecture is not as easy to relate to as art. It has
a specialist aura, and because of its high cost, only a
privileged few actually get to employ an architect at
least once in their lifetime. Yet architecture is, unlike
art, unavoidable. If art seeks an audience, architecture
seeks people. To be an audience, occasionally; to use it,
always. The London Architecture Biennale is part of a
renewed effort to regain the city for people. It surely
deserves our support.

*Robert Maxwell is professor of architecture emeritus
at Princeton University. Among his many books and
publications are* New British Architecture *(1972) and*
The Two-Way Stretch: Modernism, Tradition and
Innovation *(1996)*

Giles Worsley, 1961-2006
by Michael Hall

Writers on architecture who are both skilled historians and perceptive critics of contemporary buildings are very rare. Giles Worsley was one. When he died of cancer at the age of only 44, he was busy with a book on Inigo Jones – which will be published by Yale University Press this September – and a profile of David Adjaye for the *Daily Telegraph*, of which he was the architecture correspondent. He brought his knowledge of modern buildings to bear on his study of the architecture of the past, and vice versa.

Architecture was in Giles's blood. He was descended from an eighteenth-century amateur architect, Thomas Worsley, who designed his own house, Hovingham Hall, in Yorkshire. Giles spotted that the unusual plan of the building was modelled on that of a Roman villa nearby, which Thomas had excavated. That curiosity about an architect's motivations and influences helped to make Giles an original critic as well as a good historian. Contemporary architects were flattered and intrigued by his gentle interrogations about the books that had influenced them and the buildings they had seen and liked, of whatever date. The resulting critiques of their works moved beyond journalism in an effort to place modern design in its cultural and historical context.

In a modest way, Giles was an architectural patron himself: the arrival of three children prompted him and his wife, Joanna Pitman, to commission James Gorst to extend their north Kensington house. The result was one that was familiar to Giles from his historical studies: he did not get what he was expecting (thanks to Gorst's abrupt conversion to the Modern movement), but was delighted with the end product. He also devoted great energy and much time to his role as one of the trustees of Somerset House, helping to oversee the brilliant transformation of Sir William Chambers's monumental eighteenth-century building into a lively cultural centre for London. His early death is a loss not only to scholarship and journalism, but also to the city that was his home.

Michael Hall is editor of Apollo

London
Architecture
Biennale 2006
Change

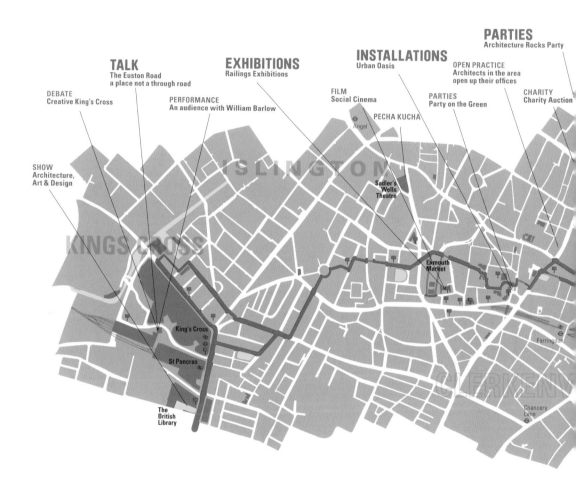

SHOW
Architecture,
Art & Design

DEBATE
Creative King's Cross

TALK
The Euston Road
a place not a through road

PERFORMANCE
An audience with William Barlow

EXHIBITIONS
Railings Exhibitions

FILM
Social Cinema

PECHA KUCHA

Angel

INSTALLATIONS
Urban Oasis

PARTIES
Party on the Green

PARTIES
Architecture Rocks Party

OPEN PRACTICE
Architects in the area
open up their offices

CHARITY
Charity Auction

ISLINGTON

Sadler's
Wells
Theatre

KINGS CROSS

Exmouth
Market

Farringdon

CLERKEN

King's Cross

St Pancras

Chancery
Lane

The
British
Library

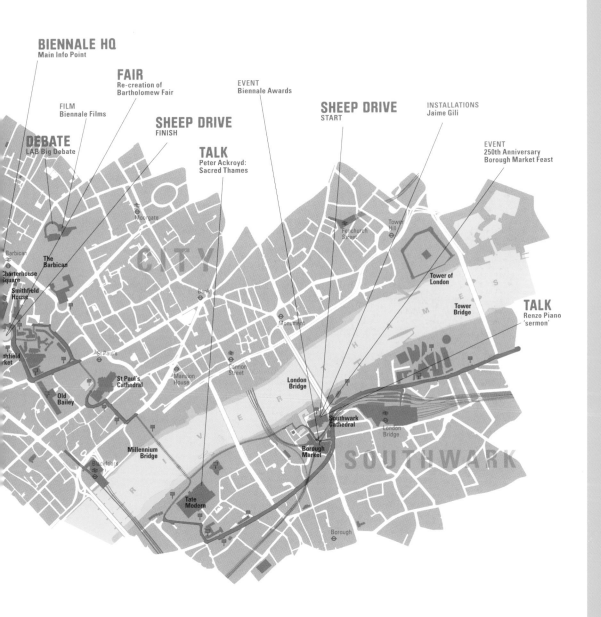

BIENNALE HQ
Main Info Point

FAIR
Re-creation of
Bartholomew Fair

FILM
Biennale Films

DEBATE
LAB Big Debate

SHEEP DRIVE
FINISH

TALK
Peter Ackroyd:
Sacred Thames

EVENT
Biennale Awards

SHEEP DRIVE
START

INSTALLATIONS
Jaime Gili

EVENT
250th Anniversary
Borough Market Feast

TALK
Renzo Piano
'sermon'

Barbican

The
Barbican

Charterhouse
Square

Smithfield
House

thfield
ket

Moorgate

CITY

Bank

Monument

Fenchurch
Street

Tower
Hill

Tower of
London

Tower
Bridge

St Paul's

Cannon
Street

Mansion
House

London
Bridge

Southwark
Cathedral

London
Bridge

St Paul's
Cathedral

Old
Bailey

Blackfriars

Millennium
Bridge

Tate
Modern

Borough
Market

SOUTHWARK

Borough

The walk route: architecture takes to the streets – King's Cross to Borough Market

Jason Bruges Studio, Creatmosphere, AIG, Benedict O'Looney, 3M

A combination of 1m and 2m diameter PVC helium-filled balloons, installed in collaboration with Creatmosphere and tethered on some of capital's key landmarks, are the Jason Bruges Studio's strong and playful visual "markers" along the entire London Architecture Biennale walk route from King's Cross to Borough Market. Using LAB06's signature magenta colour, they act as a guide to visitors and encourage them to consider the surrounding buildings and biennale interventions.

To emphasise the route, 400m diameter dots made out of special 3M graphic film designed for exterior use are placed on pavements and road junctions, while tour guides carry balloons.

By creating such strong continuity along the route over the ten-day festival, the studio hopes to generate further interest in the event and produce a beautiful physical intervention on the London cityscape.

Above, right and overleaf: Jason Bruges Studio's "marker" system uses magenta balloons to signal the biennale walk route from King's Cross to Borough Market

Location
Biennale route
King's Cross to
Borough Market

Tours along the biennale walk route

Benedict O'Looney
Sponsored by YRM

Architecture lecturer Benedict O'Looney is leading a series of early evening walks throughout the biennale. The LAB06 north-south route through London features surprising contrasts in cityscape and history, and some of the best buildings in the UK. The walks highlight both the historic and spicy new buildings encountered along the way, taking in everything from the gritty Victorian commercial architecture in Southwark and Clerkenwell to the English Baroque splendour of St Paul's.

Top: Eric Parry's London Stock Exchange building. Middle: medieval meets Edwardian. Bottom: Temple Bar

Location
Biennale route
King's Cross to
Borough Market
London

Above: Southwark
Bridge dates from 1921

Railings exhibitions

Lovejoy, MOLAS, Farrell and Partners, Benedict O'Looney

An ambitious series of railings exhibitions has been set up along the LAB06 Walk route from Southwark to King's Cross. Exhibition boards are located on the biennale map, identified by the LAB06 logo. These mini exhibitions are intended to enhance the pedestrian experience and encourage us to engage with the surrounding urban environment, encompassing both old and new buildings.

Some buildings are of historic significance, while others are interventions in ancient settings, for example Merrill Lynch building in King Edward Street. There are new buildings in the existing streetscape and some under construction or still on paper, but soon to emerge – each has its own story, from MoreLondon to King's Cross. At each exhibition there is the opportunity to stop and consider the particular building you are viewing and its context – up and down, left and right.

There are many older buildings on the route. The Museum of London Archaeological Service (MOLAS), for example, tells us more about the history of the Globe Theatre in Southwark, Southwark Cathedral, St James' Church and St John's ▶

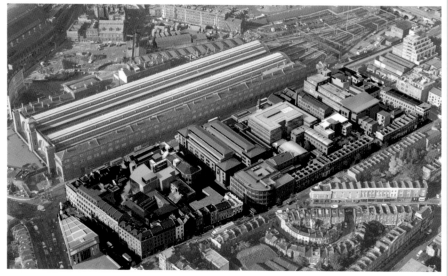

Above: Regent Quarter at Kings Cross. Right: Paternoster Square was masterplanned by William Whitfield and features buildings by McCormac, Jamieson and Prichard and Eric Parry. Left: St John Gate on St John Lane

Location
Biennale route
King's Cross to
Borough Market

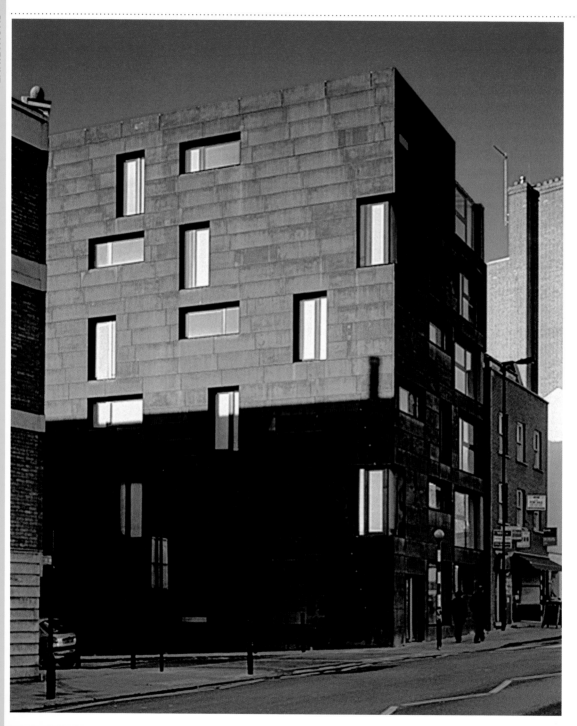

Opposite: Gazzano House in Farringdon Road by Amin Taha Architects.
Below right: approaching the Millennium Bridge

◀ Gate in Clerkenwell – what were they like when they were first built in a very different setting, and how have they changed over time?

We can admire the railings at the College of Arms in Queen Victoria Street and also learn more about the history of the building; the Marx Library has both the story of the building and of the man; the Lloyd Baker Estate is a distinctive and pretty early nineteenth-century estate built on the hills above King's Cross; St Olaf's House in Southwark is an Art Deco gem from 1932; and there are many more...

For new buildings or conversions of old ones to new uses, we are fortunate to have the story from the architects and designers themselves – what did they want to achieve and what inspired them?

At Carter Lane in the City, the Corporation of London Street Scene Challenge shares its plans for improving this key connection between the Millennium Bridge and St Paul's Cathedral.

Regent Quarter at King's Cross is the first of the major mixed-use projects in the area to be completed, and the courtyards with various art displays offer a quiet retreat from the general city bustle and traffic.

You can follow the LAB06 walk from north to south or south to north, and join or leave it at any time – and there are several resting places for a drink or snack on the way!

Bankside One: Allies & Morrison
85 Southwark Street: Allies & Morrison
Bart's Hospital: HOK
Carter Lane: City of London
Christ Church: Nicholas Boyarsky
College of Arms: College of Arms
Emap: John McAslan Architects
Farmiloes Building: Allford Hall Monaghan Morris
Finsbury Health Centre: Avanti Architects
Gazzano House: Amin

Taha Architects
The Gymnasium: Allies & Morrison
Globe: MOLAS
The Newsroom: Allies & Morrison
Haberdashers Hall: Hopkins & Partners
King's Cross St Pancras: Manhattan Loft Corporation
Lloyd Baker Estate: Amwell Society
Merrill Lynch: Swanke Hayden Connell
More London: More London Estates, Foster and Partners, Robert Townshend Landscape

Architects, Gross Max, DSDHA, Jestico & Whiles, Hawkins Brown
Museum of London: Wilkinson Eyre
Old Bailey Street Scene: City of London
Paternoster Square: sponsored by Legal & General, Mitsubishi Estates UK, Broadgate Estates and designed by Wordsearch
Peabody Estate: Peabody
Regent Quarter: RHWL, Rolfe Judd, Lovejoy
Salvation Army: Sheppard Robson,

sponsored by Hines UK and Sheppard Robson
Southwark Cathedral: MOLAS
St James' Church: MOLAS
St John's Square: MOLAS, sponsored by Dovetail
St Olaf's House: St Martin's Property
St Paul's Cathedral: Benedict O'Looney
Tate Modern: Tate Modern
Unicorn Theatre: Keith Williams Architects
Charles Rowan House: Charles Rowan House

Big London Brainstorm

Curated by Tom Dyckhoff. Designed by Piercy Conner

"An exhibition of inventions to make London, you know, a little nicer.

"Yeah, yeah, London's the best, the Olympics, urban renaissance and all that. Yes, London's getting more skyscrapers, a new King's Cross, the East London Line – good God, even Crossrail. Yes, there's (slightly) better coffee than ten years ago. But there are still estates that haven't seen a paintbrush since Maggie Thatcher turned up. You still see cruddy, cracked streets, and chain stores squeezing dusty bookshops and grocers from the high street. Ooh, and don't get me going on the Thames Gateway. London's been falling apart for centuries. Its creativity thrives on grunge and crap and chaos. But remind me of that next time I'm trying to get from King's Cross to Camberwell in under 24 hours.

"So, since we keep hearing London's the creative centre of the creative blinkin' universe – well, let's see what the creatives at the creative centre of the creative blinkin' universe can come up with. Any ideas? Any ideas to make London life, you know, a little nicer.

"'Big London Brainstorm' – at the heart of the London Architecture Biennale and its theme of change in the city – is our chance to all bang our heads together and sort out London once and for all. The exhibition, ingeniously designed by Piercy Conner, takes centre stage at the biennale hub, and, with a nod to good old-fashioned British nutty inventors such as Wallace (AND Gromit), Cedric Price, Heath Robinson, Joseph Bazalgette and Baldrick, features London's

problems picked and solved by its resident cunning creatives.

"That means any idea for any place within the M25. Buildings, of course – this is an architecture biennale, after all – but also, perhaps, a revolutionary reworking of the bollard or a new, like, ironic take on the private finance initiative. Bonkers stuff, naturally, but serious stuff too — maybe someone's innovative reinterpretation of urban life as we know it, that kind of thing. Change in the city only comes from below. Vive la revolution and all that.

"The exhibition showcases whatever they (and you, the visitor) come up with: maybe words, a back-of-the-envelope sketch, a fully completed model, a film, something recorded on their mobile phone. We don't mind. They won't be judged so much on the quality of delivery as the 'dammit, why didn't I think of that' cunningness of the solution. Ah yes, judged. The most cunning of all will be awarded rosettes, such as Best In Show, the Heath Robinson Most Bonkers Invention Award, and auctioned off for charity, which, if the prospect of making London less infuriating isn't enough to get everyone's thinking caps on, ought to give added incentive.

"And you never know, Ken Livingstone or Ruth Kelly might pop by the exhibition one lunchtime and nick one of the ideas. It might even be yours. Imagine! London's made just that little bit nicer, all thanks to your revolutionary bollard." – Tom Dyckhoff, architecture critic, *The Times*, and curator, 'Big London Brainstorm'

Location
Smithfield House
Lindsey Street
London EC1

Right: "You never know, Ken Livingstone or Ruth Kelly might pop by the exhibition one lunchtime and nick one of the ideas"

The World in a City: a Sketch for London

Curated by Matteo Cainer. Designed by New Design Research Studio at Fletcher Priest Architects Sponsored by LaSalle Investment Management

Opposite: the exhibition logo designed by New Design Research Studio at Fletcher Priest Architects

Location
The Gallery
York Way 34B
Regent Quarter
London N1

The exhibition brings the architectural world together in London on the premise of change – the theme of the biennale. With more than 70 international architectural studios from outside the UK, it consolidates the profession's role in imagining a future for the city, as each architect seeks to define a visionary project for London.

The show moves beyond the current scene, dominated as it is by cyberspace and video simulation, and beyond the familiar client restraints and the fashion parade of magazines. Instead, the intent is to privilege singularly the underestimated concept of the sketch as the fulcrum of architectural imagination, therefore envisaging a visionary response by allowing architects to conceive a project without being exposed to the usual limitations. A sketch can convey more clearly revolutionary ideas rather than developed projects.

The architects submitting a sketch are free to choose a site and focus, whether addressing issues of planning, landscape, infrastructure or building. The central challenge remains what it has been for centuries: to make architecture a vessel for new and controversial ideas.

Gathering together architects with sketches, and critics with words, in turn creates a platform for discussion and a critical examination of today's approach to architecture.

The show entices visitors into a theatre of imagination where a wide range of daring projects, conceived by some of the most inventive and newly emerging architects, form a panorama of the profession's current potential and promise.

The installation design at the newly refurbished Gallery building on York Street in the Regent Quarter, King's Cross, was commissioned from the New Design Research Studio at Fletcher Priest Architects. Participants include, among others:

From Australia: Kovac Architecture, Lab Architecture Studio and PTW Architects PTY LTD. From Austria: Berger + Parkkinen Architekten, Coophimmelblau, Gunther Domenig, Innocad, Architektura Atelier Podrecca, Propeller Z, The NEXTenterprise and Wolfgang Tschapeller. From Canada: Saucier + Perrotte Architectes . From China: Yung Ho Chang Atelier Feichang Jianzhu. From Denmark: Plot, Jds Architects and 3xNielsen. From Finland: Sanaksenaho Architects. From France: Jakob + Macfarlane, Manuelle Gautrand, ODBC Odile Decq-Benoit Cornette Architectes, Domenique Perrault Architecture, R&Sie Architects and Serero Architecture. From Germany: Zvi Hecker and Dagmar Richter. From Greece: Anamorphosis. From Holland: EEA, Erick Van Egeraat Associated Architects, NL Architects, NOX, ONL Oosterhuis Associates and UN Studio, Van Berkel & Bos. From Italy: Aldo Cibic and Partners, Massimiliano Fuksas, Metrogramma, Forsterragni, 5+1 and IAN+. From Japan: Tadao Ando Architect and Associates, Kengo Kuma & Associates, Makoto Sei Watanabe / Architects, Office, Masahiro IKEDA co. ltd, Shuhei Endo Architect Institute, Taira Nishizawa Architects and Tezuka Architects. From Korea: Studio Himma. From Mexico: LAR Fernando Romero and Rojkind Architects. From Portugal: Álvaro Siza Vieira. From Spain: Estudio Arquitectura Campo Baeza SL, Cero9, EMBT, Carlos Ferrater, Vicente Guallart Architecture, Martinez Lapea and Torres Arquitectos SL and RCR. From Slovenia: Elastik Arhitekti, Ofis Arhitekti D.O.O and Sadar Vuga Arhitekti. From Sweden: Claesson Koivisto Rune and Wingrdhs Arkitektkontor AB. From Switzerland: Anglil, Graham, Pfenninger, Scholl Architecture and Christian Waldvogel. From the United States: Ali Rahim Contemporary Architecture Practice, Archi-Tectonics, dECOi, Neil Denari, Eisenman Architects, Emergent, EOM Eric Owen Moss Architects, Evan Douglis, FO-Field Operations, Greg Lynn FORM, Studio Daniel Libeskind, Morphosis, Marcos Novak, Antoine Predock Architects Pc, RUR Architecture PC, Michele Saee, RoTo Architects, Smith-Miller+Hawkinson Architects, TEN Arquitectos, Tod Williams and Billie Tsie Architects, Bernard Tschumi Architects and Xefirotach.

Peter Ackroyd's Thames. Transition – the Thames exhibition on the Millennium Bridge

Peter Ackroyd, Bisset Adams, Wordsalad, Arup, Foster and Partners, City of London, 3M

Previous spread: Ackroyd sees the Millennium Bridge as the "perfect mid-way point on the river"

There are 106 bridges on the Thames. The oldest remaining is Newbridge, where the tributary of the Windrush joined that of the Thames; it was built in approximately 1250. The most recent, the Millennium Bridge that crosses between St Paul's and Tate Modern, was completed in 2000. Designed by architects Foster and Partners, with engineers Arup, in collaboration with sculptor Anthony Caro, it continues an ancient tradition of river crossing on this part of the Thames, linking the commerce, politics and religion on the north bank with the culture and entertainment on the south.

The Millennium Bridge is ideally situated as a mid-way point on the river, where its nature and use changes. Up stream is the young, clear river of pleasure and recreation. It flows through towns and cities, but more often through open country and some of the most beautiful parts of England. It has a history with religious and royal significance, and embodies everything that is pure and even holy about the Thames. Down stream lies the other face of the river, the darker industrial stretch. The docks, the landfill, the power stations, the factories sit among the marshes and unusable swampland. Its history is not as old on the whole, not as picturesque and wrapped up in hard labour, drudgery and anonymity.

On the west side of the bridge (looking up stream), we discuss:
- The source (the birth)
- The origin of the name (the baptism)
- The geology and topography
- The early history
- Religious activity and the holy river (the sacred lines/the offerings)
- Royal significance.

On the east (looking towards the sea), were the river grows larger, deeper and older, we deal with its darker side:
- Suicide and murder
- Crime
- Dirty water and sewage
- Disease and death
- Industry on and in the Thames
- The pool of London and docklands
- The modern history (twentieth and twenty-first centuries)
- What lies under the river.

The overall theme (linked to the location of the bridge) is of transition:
- From small stream to mighty river
- From a river of pleasure to a river of work
- From royal to civic (it lies at the beginning of the City)
- From noble river to a more malevolent river
- From west to east London
- From rich to poor
- From light to dark.

It is a river of change – changing moods, natures and uses.

Location
Millennium Bridge
London SE1

Above and left: display system designs for the Millennium Bridge exhibition by Wordsalad

Peter Ackroyd's Thames. Transition – the Thames exhibition on the Millennium Bridge

Right: Peter Ackroyd on what he calls the "darker, industrial stretch" of the Thames, to the east

The work of Dixon Jones

Curated by Deyan Sudjic. Dixon Jones, Newsroom, Guardian and Observer Archive Centre, and Parabola Land Ltd

The exhibition features proposals for the King's Place building that will house new offices for the *Guardian* and *Observer* at King's Cross in the context of other public building projects by the Dixon Jones practice.

The new project will respond to an unusual and varied brief and demonstrate an interesting and provocative attitude to public access. At ground level and below, there will be an ambitious grouping of arts-related spaces. A concert hall, seating 420, will be the focus of a diverse music programme. Designed to the highest acoustic standards, it will have the capacity to vary the acoustics to accommodate the needs of classical chamber music and every

other sort of musical and voice presentation. There will also be a rehearsal space for the two orchestras that have decided to make King's Place their new base. The Orchestra of the Age of Enlightenment and the London Symphonietta will have their offices here and use the concert hall for chamber and other smaller groupings and the rehearsal space to prepare for performances elsewhere. The formal concert hall and the more flexible rehearsal space will complement each other, providing the widest possible range of performance opportunities.

The building is located adjacent to the Regent's Canal and the impressive area of ▷

Right and far right: King's Place

Location
Newsroom, Guardian and Observer Archive and Visitor Centre
60 Farringdon Road
London EC1R 3GA

The work of Dixon Jones

Left: King's Place
features a ground floor
open to the public

◀ water known as Battlebridge Basin. The ground floor will be open to the public, with a restaurant and cafeteria next to the water. In addition to the music performance spaces, there are facilities for out-reach projects and the teaching of music. The concert hall is reached by an escalator that descends through two floors to gain access to the foyer, passing areas devoted to exhibitions of paintings, sculpture, etc.

We find it particularly interesting that the developer and instigator of this project sees the office building in an original and inclusive manner. Rather than holding the public at bay with elaborate control systems, the ground floor, lower floors and waterside will welcome them. This provides a challenging model in relation to the future Argent projects on the King's Cross site.

In chronological order, the other Dixon Jones projects are at the Royal Opera House, the National Portrait Gallery, Somerset House, the National Gallery and Exhibition Road. Each involves working with aspects of existing major public institutions. The Royal Opera House creates a "city within a city" on a whole block of Covent Garden with the purpose of preserving the much-loved auditorium. The National Portrait Gallery provides a radical new way of moving vertically that redefines the circulation system of the institution as a whole. The work at Somerset House includes the fountains and an ongoing masterplan. At the National Gallery, new circulation spaces and facilities at ground-floor level make use of existing entrances off the new pedestrian area of Trafalgar Square and, in addition, open up and reshape the spaces associated with the main portico entrance. Exhibition Road is an exercise in redefining an internationally important cultural and educational area of London. By fundamentally reassessing the relationship between cars and pedestrians in favour of the pedestrian, it will be possible to make a new kind of urban space. The purpose will be to give both a new identity and convenient access to the fifteen nationally important institutions associated with Exhibition Road.

The Southwark Effect

EXHIBITIONS

*Designed by
thomas:matthews*
*Sponsored by
Southwark
Council*

This exhibition displays and celebrates the diverse architectural elements of Southwark, London's oldest borough – from its early Modernist houses to the large-scale regeneration programmes under pay.

Highlighting the pioneering aspect of area's architectural identity, 'The Southwark Effect' features buildings from the past 100 years and ones to appear over the next ten. The journey begins with early Modernism (for example, Lubetkin's Six Pillars house in Dulwich) and projects into the future with top-class schemes that will soon emerge, including The Shard and London Bridge House by Renzo Piano and Zaha Hadid's Architecture Foundation building. Along the way, it looks at municipal housing estates from the 1950s and 1960s, such as Brandon, Heygate and Aylesbury; work from the 1980s, including examples from around the dockland areas; developments from the 1990s, such as Tate Modern; and more recent successes.

The exhibition aims to increase the general public's awareness of the built environment and the significant developments being made in Southwark.

Above: Lubetkin Six Pillar House, Southwark. Right: Will Alsop's Palestra building is a new Southwark landmark

Location
The Ragged School
Union Street
London SE1

Motionscape

Design and curated by Paul Campbell and Zoe Woodhead, TfL
Sponsored by TfL

'Motionscape' explores the interaction between mobility in the city and the urban fabric – the role of transport in creating the hierarchy of streets and public spaces that give London its structure, character and legibility. As the integrated transport authority, Transport for London occupies a key role in steering the evolution of the cityscape through its holistic responsibilities for the environment and public realm, as well as all public transport modes. A series of models, drawings and photographs introduce some historic, recent and current TfL projects. They demonstrate how investment in the public realm can act as a catalyst for regeneration.

TfL is custodian of a rich and diverse historic legacy of transport architecture and infrastructure – not only stations and their environs, but also numerous other buildings and a strategic road network of 560km which takes in a large proportion of the capital's landmarks, streets and squares. We have the task of preserving these public buildings and spaces for future generations. We must also maintain the highest design standards set by previous generations in the production and commissioning of new architecture and public space.

TfL works across its transport modes – tube, DLR, bus, tram, rail, river boat, cycling, walking, traffic and freight – to ensure the close integration and balancing of conflicting needs of different types of transport user, from the neighbourhood up to the city scale. We are a people-centred organisation concerned with what the transport network means to the everyday lives of those who use it; how the micro-level of the streetscape and the spaces in and around transport interchanges can help us to work towards creating the Mayor's vision of London as a city for people, a prosperous city, a fair city, an accessible city

Right and far right: Arup Associates' Millbank Pier features a striking ski slope roof

Location
Smithfield House
56 Charterhouse Street
London EC1

Changing London Schools

Curated by
The Architecture
Foundation
Sponsored by
Building Design
Partnership

The Architecture Foundation's 'Changing London Schools' exhibition is sponsored by BDP and set in the hub space of its Clerkenwell offices during the biennale. The show focuses on school designs, either completed or in progress, within the inner London boroughs since the start of the new millennium. It is accompanied by workshops with students, as well as presentations and debates concerning the roles architects will play in the development of the education and learning experience for the next generation of pupils. Projects exhibit innovative design thinking across a broad range of issues – education, spatiality, society, technology and the environment. Many are exemplars within public programmes, including Building Schools for the Future, private finance initiatives, city academies and community and faith schools. Smaller-scale schemes espousing highly creative approaches in classroom design, extension of facilities and ideas on external play space are also on display.

Above: school
design by Building
Design Partnership

Location
Building Design
Partnership Studios
16 Brewhouse Yard
London EC1V 4LJ

King's Cross as camera obscura

Minnie Weisz
Organised by
London Borough
of Camden
Supported by
P&O Developments
and London &
Continental
Railways

Right: King's Cross
gas holders as seen
through Minnie Weisz's
"camera obscura"

"The house is a nest for dreaming, a shell for imagining…" – Gaston Bachelard.

Artist Minnie Weisz approaches her subjects and her site-specific projects as an archaeologist might approach a dig. She unearths historical references to the buildings she chooses to inhabit, cataloguing these spaces in the context of history, myth and local lore.

She uses photography, projections and found material to explore the unseen narratives of the building, engaging with the present, past, real and imagined. Her application of the pinhole technique allows the building to become an eye, viewing an ever-changing outside world which is captured and recorded by the interior, and in turn awakens memories and stimulates dreams. A dialogue unfolds between Weisz's response to the subject and the subject's response to its surroundings. These processes of reflection and projection in her images raise questions about the identity of space, and of real and imagined worlds. Her rooms and buildings watch each other in silent witness and look back at us.

Minnie Weisz is a graduate of the Royal College of Art and has exhibited at Simon Finch Art, fa Projects and St Pancras Chambers, London. Her work is discussed in Yann Perreau's book *Londres En Mouvement*, Editions Autrement, 2005.

Location
Albion Stables
Regent Quarter
London NW1

Blooming St Luke's

EXHIBITIONS

Curated by Scarlet Projects in partnership with Islington Greenspace, EC1, New Deal and The Arts Council England

Graphic designer Peter Saville has been commissioned to create plant-based installations to revitalise St Luke's Garden. The project was conceived and is being curated by independent creative consultancy Scarlet Projects in partnership with Islington Greenspace, EC1 New Deal and The Arts Council England. The idea was developed by Scarlet Projects as part of an initiative to explore ways to reinvigorate public spaces.

St Luke's Garden is a much loved and well-used space. Situated behind St Luke's Church on Old Street – now the London Symphony Orchestra's Education Centre – it plays a central role in the life of the local community, providing an oasis of green within its resolutely urban surroundings. Sadly, it had been neglected in recent years and was in urgent need of care and attention.

Rather than going down the municipal planting route, we wondered what would happen if we asked local artists and designers, who have an eye for colour and form, but also know the garden well and have a genuine affection for it, to create plant-based schemes. We hoped this would bring the place alive in a surprising and sensory way. It also presented an opportunity to explore the potential of using planting in

contemporary urban design – an element of which seems to have been neglected in recent years in favour of hard landscaping.

The first installation, *The Process Garden* by Peter Saville, pays homage to the area's history as the centre of London's printing industry. He says: "I have always known Clerkenwell as London's printing district and particularly as the place for print origination, the almost magical process through which all colour images are reproduced in ink using dots of just four particular colours – cyan, magenta, yellow and black (CYMK) – which are known as the process colours. It seems appropriate to celebrate this unseen relationship with colour which is such an intrinsic part of local heritage."

The four print process colours, cyan (turquoise), magenta (pink), yellow and black, are represented by four new planting beds, each containing a diverse mixture of perennials, grasses and roses in a spectrum of related shades and tones. The variety of flowers provides dynamic sequences of colour from spring to autumn. A central bed, around which specially commissioned new seating (by locally based designers Precious McBane) is placed, blends the four colours, mimicking the printing process.

Right: Peter Saville's sketch for his plant-based installation at St Luke's Garden

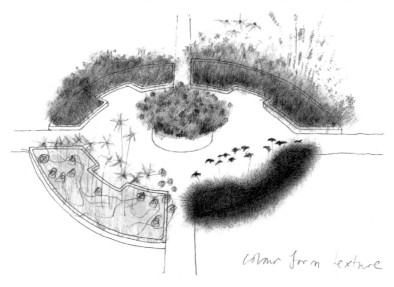

colour form texture

Location
St Luke's Garden
Mitchell Street
London EC1

Temporal Facades

Organised by
Andrew Stiff
and Nina Noor
Supported
by BDP

Temporal Facades, by Andrew Stiff and Nina Noor, consists of multiple installations of manipulated video footage captured in the biennale area projected within existing architectural structures at Brewhouse Yard, Clerkenwell. These projections are designed to enrich the urban landscape and buildings, reinvigorating elements of the city and simultaneously putting the images into a context. Themes of Terminus, Religion, Culture and Marketplaces in relation to material and dematerialised contemporary London are explored through video that combines motion and detail, colour and patterns.

Andrew Stiff is the course leader for MA Digital Arts and MA Digital Arts Online at Camberwell College of Arts, London, and a digital artist. He has recently been exhibiting videos in exhibitions in Korea and London, as well as presenting conference papers dealing with the theme of the digital environment. Examples of his work can be seen on www.stiff97.co.uk.

Nina Noor is an architect and digital artist with an interest in the built environment explored through both media. Examples of her work can be seen on www.ninanoor.co.uk/portfolio

Location
Brewhouse Yard
Clerkenwell
London EC1

Urban Carpet

Design by leit-werk
Supported by Peabody Trust and London & Continental Railways

"KingsXperience is a self-initiated project born out of the ambition to contribute to the largest urban development in our neighbourhood to date – King's Cross Central. At the time we started to work on the project, surprisingly little was discussed about the development in the public domain. As it has great potential to transform a derelict area into a vibrant part of London, we feel that local residents and businesses should be given the chance to interact and be involved in this process. The initial concept of KingsXperience proposes a temporary and flexible communication line which aims to provide information to the public during the construction. With its interventions and communication devices, it consequently encourages people to see, play, learn and experience. Once the major part of King's Cross Central has been completed the line successively becomes a permanent spatial device and infrastructure enabling urban communication on different levels and creating an aesthetic attraction.

"Putting the concept into action, making it material, we created and launched the Urban Carpet, which measures 5mx2.5m and is made of rubber and coir matting. Like a story, it conveys the existing layout of the site, while at the same time offering adults and children the chance to play hopscotch. It takes people by surprise, provoking a spontaneous reaction. The Urban Carpet has already been featured at a number of events, including the King's Cross Youth Regeneration Conference. It was partially funded by the Peabody Trust and was exhibited in the German Gymnasium.

"During the development of KingsXperience we have been in constant contact with Camden Council and the developer Argent Group, both of whom have been enthusiastically watching and backing the project. Out of this creative process with structural engineers, management and communication consultants, we transformed the Urban Carpet into a unique, accessible, tower-like sculpture, placed in the centre of the new King's Cross quarter. It is itself currently in the development stage and is defined by three main functions: communication, movement and visual surprise. The skin of the sculpture is the communication interface for information, films, art, etc, and enables direct interaction with the public. The device aims to inform and educate as well as provide special views on different levels, involving the local community, addressing their needs and supporting them during a period of intense change in their area.

"By generating new ways to look, experience and use the built environment, leit-werk provokes and stretches the confines of the conventional discourse on art, architecture and city planning. For the biennale we have been invited by Camden Council to exhibit the Urban Carpet in context with the further development of the project. It will go on show in front of St Pancras Station near the German Gymnasium. Its encounter with the public will be televised on departure screens within St Pancras Station, confronting passengers with the arrival of the Eurostar here in 2007, which is the trigger of King's Cross Central."

Location
The Gymnasium
Pancras Road
London NW1 2TB

The Urban Carpet
conveys the existing
layout of the site as well
as allowing creative play

London Loves the Thames

Gordana Korolija Fontana-Giusti, Agora team Innovation Centre, Central Saint Martins, Wordsalad, Claystation

The multimedia 'London Loves the Thames' exhibition illustrates the Agora: Cities for People research project that is concerned with the planning and sustainability of the urban environment and the relationship between cities and their inhabitants. The show encourages public participation and includes interactive displays such as a Chinese-style paper scroll for sketching and recording impressions about the South Bank, and clay modelling inviting people to create their own visions for London.

Agora: Cities for People was a three-year research project involving London, Barcelona, Malmo and Utrecht. Each research team chose a specific site within its city to explore the usability of that area, examining how the nature of urban living and impact of human activity works within the spatial context, how the cityscape affects the urban flow of people and how the existing form of the urban landscape can be improved for future usage.

The London site stretched from the Globe Theatre on the south bank of the Thames westwards along Bankside, over Hungerford Bridge towards Trafalgar Square. The main focus of research concentrated on this area of regeneration because of the growth of cultural institutions within the zone and consequent tourist activity. 'London Loves the Thames' celebrates the city's rediscovered intimacy with its river and is a statement about the sustainability of its water.

The capital has always had a profound relationship with its river. In its periods of buoyancy and social development it has reinvented itself through that relationship. This was the case in Elizabethan times, and it appears to be the case again today. After the development of the docklands and South Bank, current debate on the Thames Gateway focuses once more on London expanding along its fluvial origins.

Agora: Cities for People has been funded by the European Commission and the University of the Arts, London. It contributes to the EC Fifth Framework Programme – Energy, Environment and Sustainable Development and specifically to the objectives of the City of Tomorrow and Cultural Heritage. By developing and testing a new methodology and best practice for planning, urban design and policy making in Europe, it aims to contribute to the improvement of the quality of life in today's cities.

Future areas of focus for the urban design team at Central Saint Martins include Cities and Water and Cities and Safety. The team provides a range of urban design and planning consultancy services.

Right: 'London Loves the Thames' playfully celebrates the city's relationship with its river. Overleaf: strolling by the Thames

Project Architect:
Gordana Korolija
Fontana-Giusti
Agora Research Team:
Professor Martin
Woolley Stefan
Kueppers, Nikolaos
Koronis, Abdul
Mohammed, Wendy
Ciriello, Vineet
Choudhary, Suha Bekki
Agora Exhibition Team:
Nick Robertson, Ben
Hughes, Pier Paolo Inga
Consultant Architect:
Ranieri Fontana-Giusti

Structural Engineer:
Neil Thomas,
Atelier One.
Thanks to:
BA Theatre: Design for
Performance students
Lakin Mors and Garance
Marnier; Sylvia
Backemeyer and
Catherine Pound of the
Central Saint Martins
Museum and Study
Collection; and Jane
Rapley, Jeff Daniels,
Monica Hundal and
Thembi Morris-Hale.

Location
Bankside Gallery
(next to Tate Modern)
48 Hopton Street
London SE1 8JH

Contemporary jewellery, metalwork and textiles inspired by architectural forms

Lesley Craze Gallery

Lesley Craze Gallery has established a reputation as one of Europe's foremost contemporary jewellery galleries. To coincide with the London Architecture Biennale it is showing the work of fourteen international contemporary jewellery, metalwork and textile artists inspired by architecture. This exhibition examines the various ways in which designers take inspiration from architectural materials, processes, concepts and forms, displaying some of the freshest British talent alongside established artists with an international reputation. It brings together a diverse mix of disciplines and techniques to form a unique showcase for cutting-edge contemporary applied art. A selling exhibition with free admission, it features Vicky Ambery-Smith, jewellery; Elaine Bremner, textiles, UK; Helen Carnac, metalwork, UK; Joël Degen, jewellery, UK; Dorothy Erickson, jewellery, Australia; Anne Finlay, jewellery, UK; Gwen Fisher, jewellery/objects, UK; Sally Greaves-Lord, textiles, UK; Jennifer Haston, jewellery, UK; Chris Mullins, metalwork, Australia; Felicity Peters, jewellery, Australia; Katja Prins, jewellery, The Netherlands; Linda Robertson, silversmithing, UK; and Georgia Wiseman, jewellery, UK.

Left: mass-produced components often inspire crafted jewellery and metalwork

Location
Lesley Craze Gallery
33–35a
Clerkenwell Green
London EC1R 0DU

Onward and upward!

*Munkenbeck+
Marshall and
Jerwood Space*

Jerwood Space was the first capital initiative of the Jerwood Foundation. A Victorian school in Bankside was refurbished to create spaces for theatre and dance rehearsals. A "Robin Hood" policy enables young, emerging talent to afford the same facilities as the major companies and commercial producers, who are charged the market rate. It opened in 1998, and also has a public restaurant and contemporary art gallery with a year-round exhibition programme.

Architects Munkenbeck+Marshall will create new rehearsal spaces and meeting rooms at the top of the building, restoring space lost to bomb damage in 1940. The largest space is 16x18 metres, twice the size of existing studios. Next door is a studio for small-scale theatre and a second storey offers two rooms for auditions, casting and meetings, with balcony and city views. An additional lift will cope with bigger sets and props, and the whole building will benefit from a new air-cooling system and improved soundproofing. Rehearsals will commence again in autumn and the project will be complete in January 2007. The café and gallery will remain open to the public throughout the building work.

Director Richard Lee says: "Jerwood Space is a unique initiative, created to provide excellent space for 'the work of art'. Munkenbeck+Marshall's vision will enable us to provide more wonderful space for the capital's performing talent and business sector. Since Paxton Locher Architects carried out the original refurbishment in 1998 and Satellite Design Workshop created the Glasshouse in 2003, Bankside has seen even more architectural activity. We're delighted to be part of that exciting growth."

Alfred Munkenbeck describes the extension: "It is a lightweight steel frame construction sheathed in perforated Corten steel panels and frameless glass, chosen to contrast with the existing brick elevations. Over time the Corten will weather to a tone similar to aged brick. The final storey of frosted and clear glass will be hardly noticeable in the day against the sky, but will give a visible warm glow in the evening.

"Mechanically operated full-height timber louvres will shield the glazed end elevations from the glare of the rising and setting sun. When an indoor lever is switched, the shutters move in unison to follow the sun's path. Through external shading and increased insulation, the project will lose or gain relatively little energy, while maintaining a high degree of glare-free natural lighting.

"The structure was dictated by the very stringent acoustics required to separate musicals from Pinter, for example. The floor of the rehearsal studio is lifted on rubber mounts with longspan concrete planks so it doesn't make contact with the existing roof below. The new roof uses deep pattern galvanised corrugated steel which can span 12m from truss to truss and be left exposed as a visible ceiling."

Left: model for
Munkenbeck+Marshall's
Jerwood Space extension

Location
Jerwood Space
171 Union Street
London SE1 0LN

SAVE Britain's Heritage 1975–2005: thirty years of campaigning

Designed and curated by SAVE Britain's Heritage
Supported by Alan Baxter and Associates

Above: Smithfield Market. Right: the Royal Aircraft Establishment at Farnborough, rescued for the nation by SAVE

First shown at the V&A, this exhibition charts the progress of the campaigning charity SAVE Britain's Heritage since its inception in 1975 following the 'Destruction of the Country House' display at the V&A in 1974. It illustrates the battles won and lost for the whole gamut of the nation's architectural heritage, always with the emphasis on re-use – from country houses to churches, court houses to pubs, power stations to mental hospitals and wind tunnels to warehouses.

Location
The Gallery
77 Cowcross Street
London EC1M 6EJ

Avanti Architects – 25 years

This exhibition is a review of the themes and projects which have shaped Avanti Architects over the past 25 years. From restoring the Penguin Pool at London Zoo to building the ACAD Centre at Central Middlesex Hospital – how did we get here? What do a 28sqm keyworker studio and a multimillion-pound office development have in common?

In 1981 Margaret Thatcher was Prime Minister, *Raiders of the Lost Ark* was filmed and four London housing association architects set out on their own. Avanti Architects was born, and 25 years later a group of some 65 people from eighteen different countries, speaking fourteen different languages, continues to practise under the same collective title.

Sketches, plans, models, photographs, texts and objects explore the journey of one architectural practice.

Above: First Place
children and parents'
centre at Burgess Park

Location
Avanti Architects
361–373 City Road
London EC1V 1AS

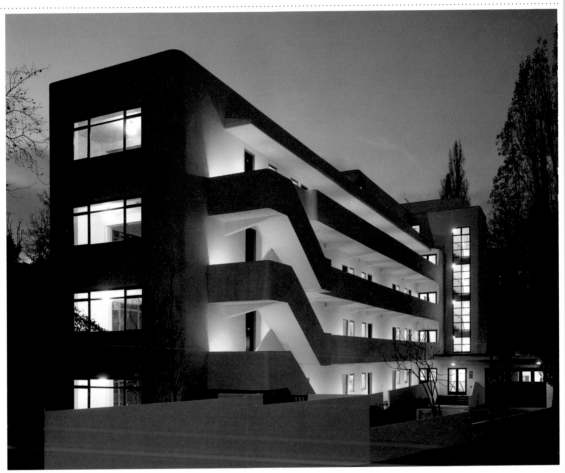

Above: the Lawn Road
flats by Isokon, restored
by Avanti

Anatomy of Engineering exhibition

*Designed by
Piercy Conner*

*Sponsored by
Price & Myers
3D Engineering*

This exhibition explores the design evolution of a dozen extraordinary structures, including buildings, bridges, stadia and sculptures. It demonstrates the exciting built environments that can be achieved with leading architects and artists by harnessing the power of advanced parametric 3D modelling.

Rapid prototyped models of the structures spin slowly in space, glowing under ultra-violet light. A short film tracing the development of the design from concept through to final construction accompanies each project.

The exhibition is most effectively shown in dark, atmospheric locations, which, for the biennale, is the House of Detention in Clerkenwell. Sans Walk, Clerkenwell, has been the site of a prison for more than 300 years.

The House of Detention itself is Victorian. Though largely demolished in 1890, the perimeter wall, warden's residence and basement level of the vast catacomb of underground cells remain. Some of these were used in the Second World War as air-raid shelters. Others were bricked up when it was a prison and have not been entered since, which no doubt contributes to its reputation as one of Britain's most haunted buildings.

The structures chosen for the exhibition in the past have included the Spiral Café at the Birmingham Bullring, the Temple Quay 2 Bridge in Bristol, the *Angel Wing* sculpture in Islington and the De La Warr Pavilion bandstand in Bexhill on Sea.

Visitors' responses:

"Really fab – well done P&M3D! They really do look like jellyfish." (Bev Dochray, Niall McLaughlin Architects)

"Good exhibition showing off cutting-edge engineering." (David Bennett)

"Interesting and exciting fusion of engineering and art." (Ruth Tilley)

The press:

"One of this year's most compelling design shows." (Fay Sweet, *Evening Standard*)

"Rapid prototyping and 3D design have never looked as so glamorous as at the 'Anatomy of Engineering' exhibition by Price & Myers 3D Engineering." (*Architects Journal* website)

"[Stuart] Piercy and [Tim] Lucas present the art of engineering in such a seductive way that it becomes a celebration of form-finding, while putting technology in its place." (David Littlefield, *Building Design*)

"It may be nothing but geometry, but what's surprising is that the result seems so beautiful and artistic." (Peter Kelly, *Blueprint*)

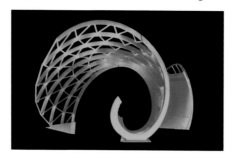

Left: model of Spiral Café at the Birmingham Bullring. Right: model for the *Angel Wing* sculpture, Islington

Location
The House of Detention
Sans Walk
London EC1

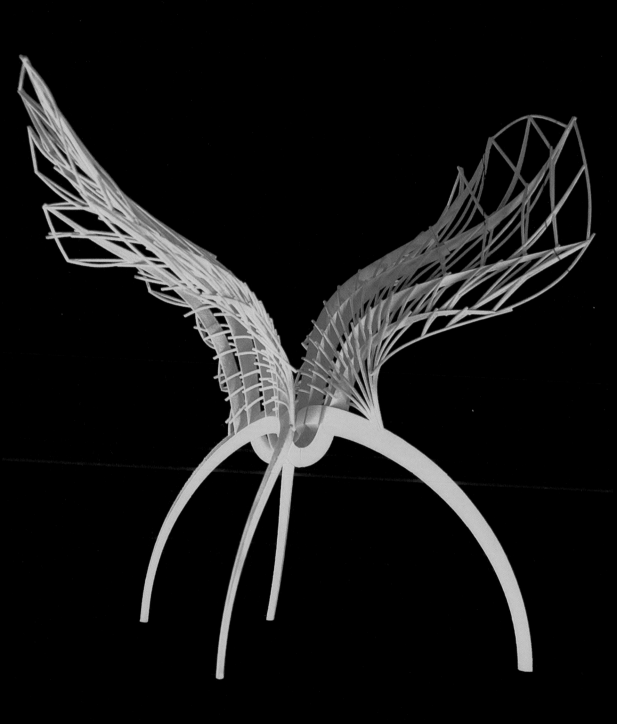

The Clerkenwell Commons Programme – The Water Clock

Designed and curated by Mike Franks, The Regeneration Trust

If a place is a space with meaning, the four linked but fragmented spaces at the heart of Clerkenwell barely qualify, despite considerable potential. The St James open space is threadbare, Clerkenwell Green is a traffic roundabout, the Clerks' Well is both inaccessible and invisible and St John's Square is almost overwhelmed by through traffic.

Walking through and around Clerkenwell Green is a haphazard experience more akin to an obstacle race. Yet in its wider urban design context this historic "commons" and its adjacent open areas are the hub of a set of pedestrian desire lines that form key parts of long pedestrian trackways running west to east from Holborn to Spitalfields, with a spur down to Farringdon Station. A major north-south axis starts on the South Bank, crosses the Millennium Bridge, reaches up the processional steps to St Paul's and then through St Bartholomew's, Smithfield, and on to St John's Gate, through Jerusalem Passage and into the Green. From there it goes north-east through Clerkenwell Close, Spa Fields, Rosebery Avenue and Sadler's Wells to the Angel, and north-west to Pentonville and King's Cross.

Historic Clerkenwell has four boundaries the youngest of which is two thousand years old. The Glacial Ridge formed by an earlier inter-glacial Thames - perhaps 200,000 years ago; the fast flowing 'River of Wells' springing out of the Hampstead Ridge that deteriorated into an open sewer - formed during an earlier inter glacial; the neolithic trackway that became the cattle drive of St John's St. in the medieval period and youngest of all Smithfield (smooth field) itself that started as a horse fair after the Crusades. Clerkenwell's well-drained gravel plateau was then ideal for the establishment of a Norman Priory and a very rich Nunnery....

Location
Clerkenwell Workshops
31 Clerkenwell Close
London EC1

Reinventing the Bike Shed

Run by Blueprint magazine in collaboration with the Design Against Crime Research Centre, Feilden Clegg Bradley Architects, Sogol Architects and Southwark Cyclists

Challenged with turning inner-city bike parking solutions into functioning objects of beauty, wonder and delight, this exhibition includes entries from the UK Student Design Competition as the first phase of *Blueprint* magazine's Reinventing the Bike Shed competition. The open competition, launched on Sunday 18 June with a public seminar, is looking for new and inventive ideas for bike storage in public spaces, workplaces and the home. Run in conjunction with CABE.

Location
Tooley Street Arches
(access via
On Your Bike)
52-54 Tooley Street
London SE1 2SZ

The Ante-Pavilion

*David Morley
Architects with
Price & Myers 3D
Engineering*
*In collaboration
with Tom Dixon
and Martyn Ware*

The Ante-Pavilion, produced by David Morley Architects, is a response to the forthcoming Venice Architecture Biennale in September. The British Council controversially chose to exclude all London-based projects from the British Pavilion at the event, resulting in an outcry from the capital's prolific architecture community.

David Morley Architects believes that it is invaluable for the city's practices to have an opportunity to flex their architectural muscles while exploring London, home to the highest concentration of architects per square foot anywhere in the world. The Ante-Pavilion asks what London's architecture community thinks of the British Council's plans for Venice, and invites all architects to "tag" the temporary structure aurally. Located at St James' Church on Clerkenwell Close, just off Clerkenwell Green, for the duration of the London Architecture Biennale, it offers the ideal resting point at the heart of the LAB route. Produced with Price & Myers 3D Engineering, it includes collaborations from Tom Dixon and Martyn Ware to create a multi-sensory and experiential pavilion.

Above: the Ante-Pavilion by David Morley Architects

Location
St James' Church
Clerkenwell Close
London EC1R 0EA

Madder Rose

*Flora Fairbairn and
Angus Maguire,
Madder Rose*
*In association with
Lynch Architects*

Situated on what is believed to be the original site of the sixteenth-century Fortune Theatre in the medieval market of Whitecross Street, London EC1, new contemporary gallery Madder Rose is directed by curators Flora Fairbairn and Angus Maguire, under the ownership of art collector Debbie Carslaw. It showcases emerging artists from the UK and abroad, while working with more established artists on large-scale curated projects both on and off-site.

Lynch Architects, Young Architects of the Year for 2005-2006, has developed the gallery from two adjacent early Georgian houses, providing a variety of dramatic split-level spaces. On the ground and basement floors there are three distinct areas, each offering its own way in which to view art: a tall sunken space with "cold" natural light; a low timber-lined "front parlour"; and a grand, "warm" top-lit hall. They can be considered as archetypal settings for art, spanning all interdisciplinary media. The diversity of spatial conditions makes visible a charged relationship between the artworks and the gallery, offering artists and curators a variety of different challenges and opportunities to think outside of the conventional "white cube".

The inaugural exhibition features a group of new sculptures by Rachel Kneebone. Working solely in porcelain, she produces large-scale yet delicately crafted figurative scenes drawn from ancient Greek and Roman myths in Ovid's *Metamorphoses* and other classical cycles. These flamboyant white sculptures of wild Bacchanalian dances, created in the seductive and lustrous material, provide a fascinating juxtaposition to the minimalist rubric of the architects' interior design.

Kneebone's recent exhibitions include 'The Way We Work Now', Camden Arts Centre; 'Young Masters', St John Street; and 'Arrivals', Pump House Gallery. A graduate of the Royal College of Art in 2004, she was shortlisted for the MaxMara Prize in 2005, and was commissioned by Mario Testino for an ongoing exhibition at Kensington Palace, London.

Left and below: model
and perspective for
Madder Rose gallery,
designed by Lynch
Architects

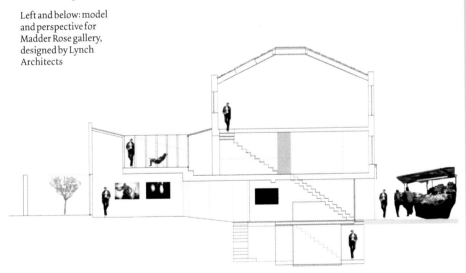

Design inspiration – Euston Underpass

*British Land and
Terry Farrell and
Partners*

*In collaboration
with EDCO,
Squint Opera and
South Camden
Community School*

Pupils of South Camden Community
School (SCCS) worked with Terry Farrell
and Partners architects, EDCO landscape
designers and Squint Opera during their
Enterprise Week. Fifteen children aged
fourteen were inspired to think outside the
box and produce ideas on redesigning the
Euston Underpass. The project placed
particular emphasis on reducing traffic
noise by using a mixture of landscaping and
architectural design. Their film, produced

with the help of Squint Opera, shows their
proposals coming to life. The project has
been structured to give them an insight into
thinking like an architect, using different
kinds of materials and communicating their
ideas in an imaginative way. British Land,
an executive of which is a governor at the
school, has been working with SCCS on
different levels, including arts projects
during the summer holidays.

 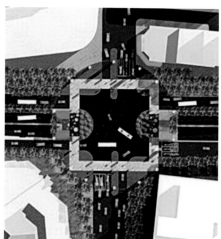

Location
The British Library
St Pancras
96 Euston Road
London NW1 2DB

Golden Lane Stories

Curated by Yanki Lee and Alan Lam of Exhibit
In association with architects Hilary French and Fred Scott

'Golden Lane Stories' is a sequel to the Golden Lane Estate exhibition mounted at the 2004 London Architecture Biennale with Chamberlin, Powell & Bon.

The first phase of the Golden Lane Estate was completed in 1957 and comprises 557 flats and maisonettes. Located adjacent to the Barbican, it is recognised as a site of special architectural and historical interest and was Grade II listed in 1997. The nature of the residency changed in the 1980s, when the key worker social housing scheme was privatised. More and more young professionals moved in, including many from the design world, attracted by its architectural character and quality design. This combination of new and original residents makes it a dynamic community with a spectrum of different social classes, ages and backgrounds.

The 'Golden Lane Stories' show at the Exhibit Empty Space gallery includes Chamberlin's original design drawings and videos. Also, the results of a collaboration between students from RCA Design Product and the elderly residents of the estate, who talked about their lives and experiences, are displayed in the exhibition in a bid to bring about a new sense of rejuvenation.

The Exhibit gallery and retail space opened in November 2005. Its location, between a bagel shop and a Costcutter on the estate's parade of shops, is part of the inspiration to explore the interaction between the locale and artists' work. It was designed by Royal College of Art alumni Yanki Lee and Pablo Abellan. Owner Alan Lam says: "Modifications made during the life of the building have been pared back and the visual connection between the estate and Goswell Road has been restored."

Exhibit invites emerging and local artists and designers to contribute installation works to the basement gallery, Empty Space. After exhibition, they go on sale on the ground floor.

Right: the Golden Lane Estate by Chamberlin, Powell & Bon. Above right: the Exhibit Empty Space gallery in Goswell Road

Location
Empty Space
Exhibit
20 Goswell Road
London EC1M 7AA

City regeneration

Lovejoy London, RHWL and Rolfe Judd

Good design demands both talent and inspiration, but it also requires an understanding of and respect for the delivery process. The exhibition at Regent Quarter by Lovejoy London explores this process, from concept to delivery, through a wide range of case studies of completed and developing projects, both in the UK and overseas.

Meanwhile, Rolfe Judd's display at Regent Quarter focuses on mixed-use regeneration projects, which constitute a major and growing share of the practice's workload. These include large-scale residential-led regeneration projects for major housebuilders, high-profile urban improvement schemes and some of the practice's current office-led developments.

Regent Quarter is P&O Developments' regeneration scheme for four city blocks to the east of King's Cross Station. RHWL

Architects developed the masterplan for the 63,000sqm project, which provides a mix of homes, offices, shops, bars and restaurants and a 275-bed hotel. They were also the lead architect on two of the blocks.

The masterplan called for the preservation of the character of the existing buildings, while allowing for contemporary insertions. At the heart of the design process was a commitment to respond to the variety of building types on the former nineteenth-century industrial complex.

The original buildings have been repaired and restored where necessary. Moreover, Regent Quarter – once an almost impenetrable district – is now fully accessible to the public via a series of pedestrian routes that link newly created open spaces and residential courtyards with the surrounding streets.

Above: RHWL
masterplanned Regent
Quarter

Location
Regent Quarter
King's Cross
London N1

Right: Paddington
Central with
landscaping by Lovejoy
Below: Regent Quarter
by Rolfe Judd

Ruta Rota

Organised by Modus Operandi Art Consultants with Riflemaker Supported by St Martins Property Group, Platform for Art and TfL

Venezuelan artist Jaime Gili was selected by art consultants Modus Operandi to contribute to the London Architecture Biennale. His practice is inspired by Modernist public art, architecture and design from his native country. *Ruta Rota* (Broken Route) comprises two inter-related projects for the biennale route using repetitive imagery: a poster series for 250 bus shelters across the four boroughs, punctuated by an installation at 5 Cheapside.

The images for each project are configured to the scale of their architectural starting point, from the grand mass of the Cheapside building to the human scale of the bus shelter. The posters, located in sites normally inhabited by advertising, are part of a series Gili intends to develop in the future for the interior and exterior of London buses, inspired by the specially designed motifs spray-painted on to buses in Venezuela. These motifs act as colourful talismans, represent speed and technological success, and calibrate the city in surprising and variable ways.

Gili's juxtaposition of black, white and coloured geometrical forms draws on the ad-hoc appropriation of Modernist ideas and their translation into different contexts. He is not interested in pastiche and the critical revisiting of Modernist design, but rather in its contemporary affirmation. He says: "I grew up in Caracas surrounded by optical art by twentieth-century masters which interacts beautifully with the city's informal architecture, inspiring the popular abstract imagery used on local buses. In *Ruta Rota* I wanted to recall a similar experience in London for bus travellers and passers-by."

Gili was born in Caracas in 1972 and is currently based in London. He studied painting at the Royal College of Art (1999–2001) and completed a PhD at the University of Barcelona. His recent exhibitions include 'Villa Jelmini – the complex of respect' at the Kunsthalle Bern (2006), a solo show at Riflemaker Gallery, London (2006) and an installation *7 x 7* for Selfridges in London. Other recent projects include *Tipos Moviles*, a collaboration with artist Luis Romero for an ongoing series of poster books featuring a selection of artists' work from the UK and South America. He is represented by Riflemaker, London.

Modus Operandi is an independent public art agency committed to promoting and supporting the vision of artists. It provides a commissioning service to a range of clients offering a lateral and creative approach to working and collaborating with artists. The range of work commissioned includes permanent and temporary art and craft, interdisciplinary collaborative schemes and artists' placements.

Organised by Modus Operandi Art Consultants with Riflemaker, with support from St Martins Property Group and TfL. Thanks to Andrew Smerdon, St Martins Property Group and Tot Taylor, Riflemaker.

Location
Various and
5 Cheapside
London EC2

Right: perspectives of Jaime Gili's poster installations for bus shelters and the windows of 5 Cheapside

Architects in public toilets – the taming of the loo

Architects in Residence

Public conveniences are becoming mythical beasts. Their misappropriation has meant that councils are more likely to shut them down than invest money. Shoppers seek out café or pub toilets, only to be greeted by a sign reading "toilets are for use by customers only". In many railway stations it costs 20p to use the loo – real inflation on "spending a penny". If the demise of public toilets is to be halted, we need to rethink how to make them places of familiarity and affection without charging punters.

A string of interventions along the biennale route focuses on the need to piss in public, highlighting both historical and contemporary uses of public conveniences. The aim is not to offer a solution, but to provoke questions about their role.

Historically, they were communal places. For the Romans, public latrines consisted of a row of continuous stone seats with no partitions. They were as much a place to gossip and debate as any Roman bath. Shared toilets were acceptable even in the private realm. In the grounds of Chilthorn Dormer Manor, a privy remains that contains a six-seater loo.

An installation on a pavement in west Smithfield, designed to question the sanctity of the toilet and the privacy expected for daily ablutions, consists of an open-air shared loo with a wallpapered wall supporting a row of urinals and toilet bowls. No privacy is afforded the users. This also serves as our main information point for the project.

It is a conundrum to make a public space private, but the familiar is often based on a memory, and memories, being personal, allow a sense of intimacy to creep into our perception of a place. With the aim of provoking a feeling of affection for the public toilet, childhood memories of domestic bathrooms are re-created by redecorating one cubicle of the West Smithfield public loos. It has been transformed by being wallpapered, carpeted and decorated with crotched toilet seat covers, bowls of potpourri, rose coloured toilet paper hidden under dolls' skirts and back issues of *Giles* annuals. Running concurrently is the idea of creating a dual use for public toilets, acknowledging the need to oversee them without open policing – so bookshelves and magazine racks line the railings leading up to the loos.

A map made for the biennale reveals the often hidden locations of public conveniences, while a redesigned set of public amenity signs placed in front of them identifies the categories into which they fall: public (council operated), semi-public (railway stations, libraries), customers-only (pubs, cafes) and private (offices, homes).

Location
Various locations
around Smithfield
Market
Charterhouse Street
London EC1A 9PQ

Right: Architects in Residence questions the sanctity of the toilet in west Smithfield

Re-cover(y)

*Architecture Sans
Frontieres UK*

Increasing population numbers, poverty, rapid growth of urban centres, global warming, natural disasters and ongoing conflicts have had a huge impact on the living conditions of millions of people across the globe over the past decade. Often they find themselves homeless and vulnerable with limited access to basic, let alone dignified, habitats. Such circumstances pose an important challenge for architects and professionals who work for the improvement and long-term development of the built environment.

Architecture Sans Frontieres UK consists of a group of architects, students and other built environment professionals concerned with exploring the role of architecture, construction and urbanism in "human development". We aim to use our skills to help to provide dignified habitats for vulnerable individuals and/or communities in Britain and abroad. This requires constant re-examination of the way we work and how we engage with those outside the profession. We are a not-for-profit organisation and, as part of the ASF international network, support the implementation of the Millennium Development Goals stated by UN-Habitat. We collaborate with local and international organisations that share our values and promote the self-sufficiency and empowerment of communities. Through research and active engagement with various projects and initiatives, we provide learning opportunities for architects and designers interested in areas of regeneration and development that are normally perceived to be outside the scope of architectural practice.

The aim of our *Re-cover(y)* installation is two-fold: it explores how people's interactions with London and its built environment are changing, and it illustrates alternative forms of practice that respond to the humanitarian agenda outlined above.

The stand is made of reclaimed materials. We have selected a number of participants to design, construct and man the installation as it develops through the course of the week – a process based on notions of heuristic learning and "reflective practice". The recording of this process becomes part of the installation itself.

Re-cover(y) promotes educational, awareness-raising information about the nature of urban settlements, development, society and sustainability. Its design and erection process attempt to illustrate some of the challenges of working with limited materials, and the benefits and results that can be obtained from an inclusive approach to design. This is intended to contribute to the debate about how the role of architecture and the way we work might be broadened to respond to the needs of those who live in vulnerable environments.

Right: *Re-cover(y)*, a shelter made from reclaimed materials by Architecture Sans Frontieres UK

Location
Vernon Square
London WC1X 9EW

The perception thing: 'A room with a view'

Design for a folly
Organised by
ORMS

To subtly, or otherwise, alter people's perceptions of the Pine Street environment; to help them to see London's buildings in a different way; provoking the engaging questions of "Why?" and "How?". That was out challenge.

Pine Street is an anonymous street which links Exmouth Market and Bowling Green Lane, and forms part of the biennale route. ORMS relocated here in 1993. It is synonymous with The Pine Street Health Centre, designed by Bertold Lubetkin in the 1930s, and also houses private residences, day centre visitors, publishers, surveyors and architectural practices.

The question we posed ourselves was: "Why would the general public want to visit the biennale, and how would we engage them with Pine Street?"

The LAB is not an architecture show for architects. It is not contained within the walls of a private gallery. It is an open-air exhibition allowing visitors to explore a series of installations/events along a route through the city. We have introduced a "moment to reflect" along the way and a chance to understand "where you have been" and "where you are going to". Our installation is interactive and is the only three-dimensional extrusion of the route.

Architects enjoy unrivalled access to many buildings in London. Our "room with a view" affords the general public stunning views across the rooftops of Clerkenwell to St Paul's, The London Eye, Centre Point and St Pancras Chambers.

We have taken the precedent of a folly (somewhat tongue in cheek), which is really a rich man's plaything. Located in the landscape of famous gardens, such as Stowe School, they are often neo-classical eighteenth-century stone buildings; a place for reflection and escape from the bustle of everyday life. Typically, they are strategically "hidden" in the landscape.

Our folly is designed for public use, on a public thoroughfare with free access, offering one of many views upon which you get a perspective on architecture as the subject. Ultimately, it provides an opportunity to reflect on how one of the smaller streets in London makes a contribution to the bigger picture.

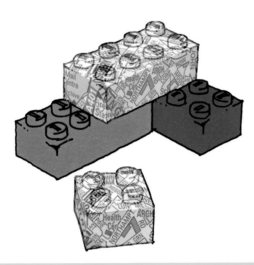

Location
Pine Street
London EC 1

93

AUNT-SUE – accessibility, urban design and inclusive transport

*Cities Institute,
London
Metropolitan
University*

AUNT-SUE (Accessibility and User Needs in Transport) is an action research project funded by the Engineering & Physical Science Research Council for Sustainable Urban Environment (SUE) programme. It is investigating and producing inclusive design solutions to mobility and transport access through urban design and user-led planning.

Test-bed sites have focused on Somerstown and Elm Village in the King's Cross/St Pancras area of Camden. Street and access audits, urban design and visualisation, community consultation and scenario building using digital mapping are producing a detailed model of access and design of the whole journey environment. Methods include ergonomic design of facilities and street layout for a wide range of physical abilities; designing out crime and fear of crime; community and transport surveys; and urban design quality assessment. Community and street surveys are also being undertaken in urban heritage sites in Homerton, Hackney, York and Salford, using a GIS-Participation tool as part of the InSITU community planning research project.

Artists-in-residence Helen Bendon and Jessica Thom are exhibiting artworks throughout LAB week, including photographic and audio-video installations based on the AUNT-SUE case study theme and sites. Architect Nastaran Azmin-Fouladi and landscape designer Vanessa Newton are also showing large-scale visualisations of the neighbourhoods using GIS mapping of social, environmental and design data and features, together with photographs of building elevations and street layouts. The exhibition interprets local people's experience and views of accessibility and movement in their urban environment.

Partners include the London Borough of Camden (accessibility planning), local community and resident organisations and the Metropolitan Police (designing out crime). Project steering committee members include the Department for Transport, Hackney Community Transport, Hertfordshire County Council and the Union of International Transport Providers, Brussels.

Local event organiser: Cities Institute, London Metropolitan University, on behalf of the AUNT-SUE and InSITU consortias, including Loughborough University Ergonomics and UCL Transport Studies departments (AUNT-SUE), and Stockholm Environment Institute, University of York and Salford University (InSITU).

Right: a visualisation of
AUNT-SUE's theme

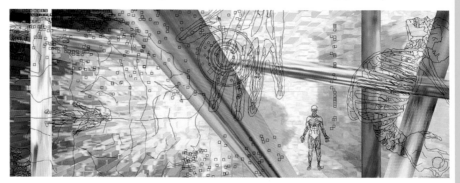

Location
The Gymnasium,
Pancras Road, London
NW1 2TB
and Somerstown
community centres

VivaCity 2020

*Cities Institute,
London
Metropolitan
University*

VivaCity is a five-year Sustainable Urban Environment (SUE) action research programme funded by the Engineering & Physical Science Research Council. The project is investigating urban design solutions to mixed-use development and city centre living at the building, street, neighbourhood and "urban village" levels.

An intensive case study has been based in and around Clerkenwell – from Hatton Garden to Bunhill – capturing and critiquing building design and layouts (vertical and horizontal mix) and undertaking surveys of householders, businesses and the development and planning sectors. Key themes include mixed-use/tenure and quality of life; street and property crime; amenities/public toilets; night-time economy; environmental quality (noise and air pollution); and housing and workspace design. Comparative mixed-use studies have also been undertaken in Sheffield and Salford, Manchester.

For the biennale, commissioned artists-in-residence Helen Bendon and Jessica Thom are exhibiting at the Hoopers Gallery, Clerkenwell Green. Based on discussions with residents about how they feel the nature of the area is changing, photographic and audio-video installations with project posters and images capture the shifting landscape of Clerkenwell, one of the first designated "urban villages", and reflect on the way we actually understand our immediate surroundings through anecdote, tall tales and fragmented narratives. As Peter Ackroyd poses in his biography of London: "If there is a continuity of life, or experience, is it connected with the actual terrain and topography of the area? Is it too much to suggest that there are certain kinds of activity, or patterns of inheritance, arising from the streets and alleys themselves?"

The artists are available to discuss their work and impressions at the gallery and project staff are presenting a series of talks on "VivaCity: continuity and change" during the biennale week.

Local VivaCity project partners include the London Borough of Islington, local community and residents associations, the Metropolitan Police (safer neighbourhoods) and a steering committee made up of the ODPM, Housing Corporation, Jill Dando Institute of Crime Science, Prince's Foundation and Urban Splash.

Local organiser: Cities Institute, London Metropolitan University, on behalf of the VivaCity consortium, which includes built environment departments at University College London, Sheffield University and Salford University.

Right: the shifting landscape of Clerkenwell as interpreted by the artists-in-residence

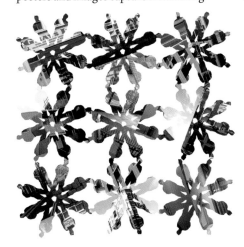

Location
Hoopers Gallery
15 Clerkenwell Close
London EC1R 0AA

London Architecture Biennale National Student Festival

Organised by Pippa Gueterbock, EDAW Supported by London Metropolitan University, archaos, Ove Arup Foundation, Fluid, The Happold Trust

Installations

The LAB Student Festival involves students from architecture and urban environment and higher education courses across the UK working with children from schools in the biennale boroughs of Camden, Islington, the City of London and Southwark. Together they have designed and built major interventions along the 5km LAB06 walking and cycling route.

The impressive installations – permanent and temporary structures – may add light, sound and colour and provide seating and shelter in public spaces along the route during the day and the night. They may be landmarks that surprise, delight and attract passers-by, as well as signposting the route. Students were asked to create designs that refer to the spatial qualities or history of each chosen site, or the way that it is used, abused or misused currently by people. They may also consider themes such as environmental impact and future of the place.

The idea of "live projects" in architectural education is important, as it gives students experience of working through real architecture-related issues such as planning and health and safety procedures and liaising with a number of different partners,

local authorities, etc. It also gives local people, schoolchildren in this case, the opportunity to be involved directly in the biennale. In the lead-up to the creation of the interventions, each group of students was mentored by professional architects, including Featherstone Associates, Penoyre & Prasad, Squire & Partners and TP Bennett.

Sites include the British Library, Argyle Square, St John's Square, Paternoster Square, Millennium Bridge Landing, Tate Beach/River Walk, Bankside Jetty, The Golden Hinde, Montague Close and Borough Market.

The following schools of architecture and design are taking part: Architectural Association, Bartlett School of Architecture, Brighton School of Architecture, Canterbury School of Architecture, Central Saint Martins College of Art and Design, London Metropolitan University, Ravensbourne College, Robert Gordon University, Scott Sutherland School of Architecture, University of Sheffield, University of East London, Westminster University.

Event: The Big Crit

Students are presenting their interventions for discussion with a panel of architects and

Right: *Houses in the Square* at Paternoster Square by students of Robert Gordon University.

Location
Sites include: The British Library, Argyle Square, St John's Square, Paternoster Square, Millennium Bridge Landing, Tate Beach /River Walk, Bankside Jetty, The Golden Hinde, Montague Close and Borough Market

the public at the Guardian Newsroom, Archive and Visitor Centre, 60 Farringdon Road, EC1R 3GA. Here are a few examples of the type of project on show:

Central Saint Martins College of Art and Design (MA Narrative Environments): Bobby Smith (aka Story Bubble)

A wayfinding project, touched with fantasy: an oversized bubblegum machine in Smithfield Market contains messages on the gumball papers written by school children, which suggest little events and tell little stories (or little fantastical lies) about the place's history.

London Metropolitan University, Department of Architecture and Interior Design: 140 Boomerangs

The spiralling roadway in west Smithfield is echoed by a helix tower placed in the central garden, drawing attention to one of London's hidden architectural gems and the biennale. A local children's clay sculpture exhibition is held in the bumpy interior of the timber structure, which wraps the "peace" fountain at the centre.

Robert Gordon University, Scott Sutherland School of Architecture: Houses in the Square

Thirty toy houses are laid out in a grid pattern in Paternoster Square. The form of the "house" is based on the archetypal Scottish "bothy", but at a scale small enough for playing in.

Kent Institute of Art and Design, Canterbury School of Architecture: Prototypical foodstuffs

St Mary Overie Dock was once used for unloading produce for Borough Market, but now holds Francis Drake's *The Golden Hinde*. One hundred "prototypical foodstuffs" are exhibited here again for the festival.

The University of Sheffield: Sand Scape

A playful interactive canopy at Montague Close linking the cathedral to the water is representative of growth and decay and the flowing river, and displays the approximate water level on the site if the Thames were to flood.

Architectural Association: The AA Social Cinema @ Scoop

For one evening in midsummer The Scoop comes alive as an extension and reflection of the Thames, by covering it with a horizontal billowing screen upon which are projected moving images speculating on the river as source, river as flow, river as change.

Left: *140 Boomerangs*, sculpture for west Smithfield by students of London Metropolitan University
Right: *Remember the River* at Cathedral Square, Montague Close, by students of Sheffield University

'Urban Oasis' by Chetwoods: a breath of fresh air for London

Laurie Chetwood, Chetwoods with Arup, WSP, Jackson Coles and Martin Bellamy

'Urban Oasis', an exciting new concept by Chetwoods architectural practice, is launched at the London Architecture Biennale as a centrepiece on Clerkenwell Green. At 7.5 metres high and using the latest photovoltaic and fuel-cell technology, it aims to restore and reinvigorate people's spirits as they go about their daily lives. The interactive and naturally powered kinetic structure is a response to the growing urban challenge of the twenty-first century. It provides cleaner air, quieter space and is totally environmentally sustainable, acting as an exemplar for the Mayor's environmental strategy for London.

Drawing on the traditional interpretation of an oasis as a place that provides rest and sanctuary in the midst of harsh, barren environments, and harnessing and recycling natural resources, it responds to the prevailing conditions – day, night, the seasons, the weather, pollution – in order to create a positive, enjoyable experience for the city dweller. It is designed to impact on all the senses – sight, sound, taste, touch and smell.

A thermal chimney helps to power a turbine and creates a cooling effect around its base during the day. This turbine is aided by a wind-powered turbine above.

Encapsulated within the chimney is a tree-like structure whose branches open and close as the sun rises and sets. They are dressed with photovoltaic panels that collect rain. The project team includes Arup, WSP, Jackson Coles and Martin Bellamy.

Chief executive Laurie Chetwood says: "'Urban Oasis' marks a return to the true sense of the word oasis, but with a fresh interpretation for the twenty-first century. Our vision is to create a new urban icon, with 'Urban Oases' adapted for each of the communities they serve and for the natural resources available."

Laurie Chetwood founded Chetwoods in 1992. It now has more than 100 employees in the UK across three offices in London, Leeds and Birmingham, has won many awards, including Architectural Practice of the Year, and was shortlisted for the Stirling Prize. Its built portfolio now exceeds £1.5bn. Inspired by natural and organic forms, he believes buildings must balance the head and heart – being at once beautiful and clever. If successful, this design approach leads to enjoyable architecture that is valuable to users and owners alike. The practice endeavours to incorporate sustainable principles – economic, social and environmental – in all its projects.

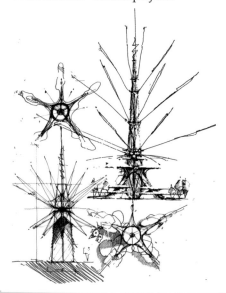

Location
Clerkenwell Green
London EC1R 0QJ

Above and left: 'Urban
Oasis', the kinetic
sculpture by Chetwoods
for Clerkenwell Green

Puss and Mew: the revival of an eighteenth-century gin vending machine

*Luis Carvajal and
Annie Davey*

Puss and Mew is an interdisciplinary arts project devised by Luis Carvajal and Annie Davey; a fiction evolving through the re-creation and reinvention of cultural artefacts and phenomena rooted in English social history, and the universal Dionysian appetite for intoxication.

Gin was regarded as the first urban drug after the "gin craze" of the early eighteenth century. The original Puss and Mew proliferated in London during the late 1730s, operating surreptitiously to avoid the notice of informers and justices of the peace. These devices demonstrated how the unpopular and ultimately unsuccessful Gin Acts could not suppress the powerful new social forces that had led to the huge consumption of gin.

First revived in Clerkenwell during the London Architecture Biennale 2004, the *Puss and Mew* – a little known architectural intervention for distributing gin – this time surfaces in historic Southwark. The transaction begins at The Ragged School with the purchase of a brass trade token, based upon those in circulation when legal tender was in short supply, from a modern token dispenser. Participants then trace a route through Southwark to the vending machine. The *Puss and Mew* dispenses a Dutch gin, or genever – the name by which the drink was historically known when first imported and distilled. Genever is served straight and is more palatable than London Dry.

Right and opposite:
Puss and Mew gin
bottle and the vending
machine in Southwark

Location
The Ragged School
47 Union Street
London SE1

Overlooked

Angela Wright

"I have chosen an intervention/installation site in a long-forgotten, sad corner of Green Dragon Court en route to Borough Market, close to Southwark Cathedral.

"This site, barricaded by a high grill/fence, holds a psychological fascination for me and sits well with the idea of change. The space is overlooked by a domestic window, giving it the feeling of a courtyard that never sees the light of day. Overhead, the massive bridge supports are awesome and bear down on my work, which, by contrast, is fragile and ephemeral.

"The installation consists of a white carpet of unfired porcelain pieces. These are stacked, supporting each other, and have echoes of a city/landscape or a thrown down fleece. The carpet will produce a luminous white floor in the gloom.

"The content of my artwork is rooted in events in my emotional life – much is fragile, easily broken and vulnerably placed, often testing the duration of its existence.

"I make constructions from multiple similar parts, which are often difficult and very time-consuming to produce. They involve repetitive actions, which can be uncomfortable and physically demanding. Works develop as studio sketches – tests and ideas are fully realised only in a suitable context.

"The work is site-specific and only reaches a final conclusion in situ. Before its installation I have no guarantee of the results. Its effects and full content remain uncertain. I walk between failure and success – this vulnerability is an essential part of my working process. I am driven by my ambition to succeed and make something happen." – Angela Wright.

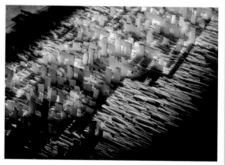

Above: The *Overlooked* site at Green Dragon Court
Above right: one of Angela Wright's environmental artworks

Location
Green Dragon Court
Borough Market
London SE1

SUB URBAN

*A-EM in
collaboration with
Alan Williams*
*Supported by ISG
Interior Exterior*

"Under the pavements, the beaches…"
As part of the London Architecture Biennale, this exhibition explores subterranean London through photography and installation. It is the result of a long collaboration between photographer Alan Williams and architects from A-EM, Glyn Emrys and Pascal Madoc Jones. Together they have researched and photographed a series of unique spaces hidden underground in the capital.

Special permissions have been granted to picture many exclusive and secret locations, which range in character from industrial cavern to private club, bank deposit room to

Victorian catacomb. Together, the images explore transgressive boundaries between light and darkness, the exclusive and the marginal, the everyday and the timeless. They reveal the city as a repository of the unconscious, evoking what Guy Debord once famously described as "the psycho geographical articulations of the modern city".

The final exhibition, also underground, is housed in a cavernous cellar, formerly a brewery, in Clerkenwell, at the heart of the biennale. It provides a unique space in which to experience and reflect on the subject and features many bespoke installation spaces.

Right: Reservoir by Alan Williams. Overleaf: safety deposit boxes in an underground vault shot by Alan Williams as part of 'SUB URBAN'

Location
187–211 St John Street
(entrance in Haywards
Place)
London EC1R 0EU

Logoland

Adrian Scrivener

Logoland is a sculpture by London-based artist Adrian Scrivener. It is a direct response to the uncompromising urban morphology of Osaka in Japan, where Scrivener spent three months during a residency.

In contrast to the prominent buildings or monuments found in older cities, which not only provide immediate landmarks for orientation, but define the character of the locality, the artist found a strange appeal in the bland, box-like buildings compressed into the Kansai basin – structures so anonymous they merge into a collective mass, an endless blanket of concrete and cladding stretching to the horizon.

Amid this man-made homogeneity, the myriad brightly coloured signs built directly and permanently into the architectural matrix of the space are the city's true landmarks. The most abstract and boldest of these symbols provide a universal alphabet essential for navigation against the backdrop of otherwise unintelligible Japanese script. *Logoland* is a map of the spatial topography of the area using this graphic language alone.

The astonishing number and variety of symbols became ever clearer as more than 1,000 different examples were photographed during three months of exploration in the region. Representing everything from large corporations to schools and temples, the resulting catalogue celebrates the inherent beauty in their design, and confirms Japan as a highly visual culture that places great faith in the effectiveness of abstract imagery to convey meaning.

As part of the process of construction, relevant logos were redrawn on the computer, outputted as printed panels and

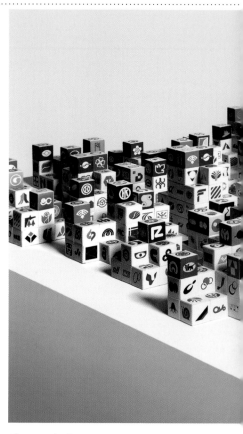

Above: *Logoland* sculpture by London-based artist Adrian Scrivener

Location
124–132
Clerkenwell Road
London EC1

finally assembled to create autonomous cuboid structures – all spatially representing the particular district from which they had originally been collected. Lightweight, hollow and made entirely of card, they reflect modern prefabricated construction, and are reminiscent of the more ancient practice of origami.

In the completed *Logoland*, the modular building blocks interlink to echo the peculiar sprawling, low-level morphology of the region as a whole – suggesting a miniature city of pure sign.

The exhibition for the biennale is the first showing of the project outside Japan. It has taken two years to complete.

Stand here for clean air

Elegant Embellishments
Supported by Millennium Chemicals (a Lyondell company)

Elegant Embellishments, in collaboration with Millennium Chemicals (a Lyondell company) is contributing two installations to the London Architecture Biennale. Each is composed of decorative, three-dimensional architectural tiles that can be installed quickly near roads to reduce levels of nitrogen oxide, a key contributor to air pollution in urban environments. They provide councils, developers and designers with the ability to improve urban environments rapidly in terms of air quality and visual appeal.

Set within the context of street and pedestrian traffic in St Bartholomew's Fair, a tiled screen marking the St John Street entrance acts as a recognisable and effective de-polluting filter between pedestrian and vehicular zones. A second freestanding structure in the market area demonstrates reclamation of a space in the city, signalling to the public that the immediate air is safer to breathe.

Elegant Embellishment's tiles can effectively improve air quality by reducing nitrogen oxide in localised areas within cities to help to support the priorities set by the EU Clean Air Strategy 2005. The goal of this policy is to reduce pollution-related deaths by more than 100,000 and air pollution-related damage by up to 45 billion Euros annually. Emissions from combustion engines are identified as the largest contributor to air pollution in cities and often invisibly affect our breathable air. The tiles, when positioned near pollutant sources, have been found to reduce nitrogen oxide levels, a contributing source of ground-level ozone and smog, and can help to reappropriate these polluted spaces for safer pedestrian use.

Millennium Chemicals supplies the active ingredient, a specific form of ultra-fine titanium dioxide (TiO_2), which is formulated into a proprietary coating and applied to the tiles. In this instance, through the photocatalytic activity of the TiO_2, atmospheric pollutants such as oxides of nitrogen (NOx) are neutralised by the specially treated tiles. There are many other applications in which the functional properties of photocatalytic TiO_2 can be exploited to render surfaces de-polluting, self-cleaning and anti-microbial.

Raising public consciousness is as necessary a proponent for social change as the de-polluting quality of the tiles. Their presence signals to the public that the immediate air is safer to breathe and may help to instil a new sense of ownership in degenerate areas. They also respond directly to a need to find appropriate architectural expression for a whole class of new high-performance "smart" materials. The tiles incorporate sophisticated processes that occur on a molecular, invisible level and are radical enough to transform our conceptions of buildings.

Location
St John Street and west
Smithfield
London EC1A 9HY

Right and below: the
Elegant Embellishments
sculptural installations
are made of tiles which
reduce levels of nitrogen
oxide

Gates of the City

COMPETITION

Organised by Southwark Council
Sponsored by Land Securities

Gates of the City, an ideas competition inviting students from local secondary schools to submit possible designs for the interior of the Great Guildford Street Tunnel, has been sponsored by Southwark Council as part of its contribution to the London Architecture Biennale. While there is currently no commitment to implement the designs of the winner – announced at the LAB Renzo Piano "sermon" – Southwark hopes to secure section 106 funds to bring them to fruition. These and the shortlisted schemes are exhibited during the LAB at The Unicorn Theatre. There are also prizes for the school and participants. The intention is to encourage young people in Southwark to promote an awareness of and interest in architecture and become involved in the development of their surrounding built environment. Architectural practices, including Panter Hudspith, Architecture plb, Spacecraft and The Facility Architects, have supported the project and visited the schools to hold workshops.

Location
The Unicorn Theatre
147 Tooley Street
MoreLondon
London SE1 2HZ

Reinventing the Bike Shed – launch and seminar

COMPETITION

Run by Blueprint in collaboration with the Design Against Crime Research Centre, Feilden Clegg Bradley Architects and Southwark Cyclists

Reinventing the Bike Shed is an open competition that is searching for new solutions to inner-city bike parking in public spaces, workplaces and the home. The seminar is intended to kick-start innovative thinking with contributions from *Blueprint* magazine, bike theft researchers, designers, architects and planners. We're looking for inventive solutions on any scale and for any end, from a one-off locking device in your backyard to a large-scale "bike shed".

There are two categories:
Serious solutions – practical proposals that could go into production.
Pushing the boundaries – extreme or eccentric ideas that challenge current thinking.

Location
Tooley Street Arches
(access via
On Your Bike)
52–54 Tooley Street
London SE1 2SZ

Redesigning the Public Convenience – flushed with ideas

Organised and funded by Southwark Council
Supported by RIBA Journal

The winning entry in this "ideas" competition aimed at architectural students and practices to redesign two disused public convenience sites within Southwark at Grange Road and Tooley Street is displayed during the LAB at The Unicorn Theatre. With the *RIBA Journal* as media partner and organised by Aitken Leclercq on behalf of Southwark Council, the objective of the competition is to celebrate the architectural possibilities of both sites and raise the profile of architecture in the borough, concurring with the LAB theme of change.

Location
The Unicorn Theatre
147 Tooley Street
MoreLondon
London SE1 2HZ

Future City: Experiment and Utopia in Architecture 1956–2006

Barbican Art Gallery in partnership with Clifford Chance
Supported by bd

From extraordinary houses and incredible towers, to fantasy cityscapes and inhabitable sculptures, 'Future City' showcases 70 of the most radical and experimental architectural projects of the past 50 years which have challenged convention to shape and influence the way we live.

Location
Barbican Art Gallery
Barbican Centre
Silk Street
London EC2Y 8DS

Renzo Piano 'sermon'

Organised by
Southwark
Council
Supported by
Southwark
Cathedral

Internationally acclaimed Italian architect Renzo Piano's talk – or " sermon" – at Southwark Cathedral effectively opens the biennale. After graduating in 1964, he spent five years travelling in the UK and America to complete his studies. In 1971 he founded the Piano and Rogers practice with Richard Rogers, his partner for the Centre Pompidou project in Paris, and in 1977 went on to set up l'Atelier Piano and Rice, working with Peter Rice on many major projects.

The Renzo Piano Building Workshop now has offices in Paris and Genoa with about 100 employees, including architects, engineers and specialists. Recent jobs include The Morgan Library in New York and The Shard development, which has received planning permission at London Bridge.

Above: Renzo Piano, the architect of The Shard development, right

The Big Debate: what skyline does London want?

*Organised by
The Architecture
Foundation*
*Supported
by Barbican
and The Zetter*

Top: Lee Polisano.
Middle: Farshid
Moussavi. Above:
Adam Caruso.
Right: Rem Koolhaas

London's skyline is about to be transformed forever as a series of ever-taller buildings spiral upwards over the next few years. Current policies will result in its redesign, but what will it look like? Do we want – or indeed need – more tall buildings? How much influence should the Mayor wield over planning proposals, and have the people who live and work in London been fully consulted? Do we want more "gherkins" sprouting up across the city, and do we risk changing forever views which form London's unique heritage? A panel of leading architects and opinion-formers addresses these issues in The Big Debate.

The debate features acclaimed international architect Rem Koolhaas and is chaired by Rowan Moore of The Architecture Foundation. Other speakers include Farshid Moussavi (Foreign Office Architects), Adam Caruso (Caruso St John Architects) and Lee Polisano (KPF).

This event is held in association with the 'Airspace' exhibition hosted by The Architecture Foundation, taking place between 9 June and 14 July in Regent's Place NW1. 'Airspace' presents specially commissioned visualisations by Cityscape, which illustrate potential scenarios for London's skyline, and explores the issues and implications of future visions of the capital.

Location
Barbican Theatre
Barbican Centre
Silk Street
London EC2Y 8DS

Blueprint Big Breakfasts

Organised and supported by Blueprint

Sponsored by Cundall, Pipers, Collyer Bristow, Kingston Smith, Austin-Smith: Lord

TALKS, SEMINARS & DEBATES

With a line-up of well-known and fearlessly outspoken speakers – as well as extremely tasty food – the Blueprint Big Breakfasts are again one of the highlights of the London Architecture Biennale.

Held at Smiths of Smithfield restaurant in east London, there are five breakfasts from Monday to Friday, 8.30–9.30, each focusing on the specific concerns of our five impassioned Londoners and providing a hearty and entertaining start to the day.

Janet Street-Porter

The architecturally-trained, opinionated commentator and editor-at-large of the *Independent on Sunday* returns with more personal reflections on the capital's architecture. Always unpredictable – at a Big Breakfast two years ago she criticised David Adjaye's work on her house in Clerkenwell, and called Stephen Bayley a tosser.

Location
Smiths of Smithfield
Charterhouse Street
London EC1M

Alain de Botton

The best-selling writer and philosopher has recently turned his sharp eye on the built environment with a new book, *The Architecture of Happiness*. For the Big Breakfast he provides a critique of modern London, arguing that its development has gone badly wrong since the nineteenth century, turning it from "a beautiful Georgian city into a monstrous ill-planned sprawl".

Simon Jenkins

In recent years this respected journalist and commentator has written frequently in *The Times* and the *Guardian* on design and the built environment – recently labelling Modernism as "odious utopianism" and arguing that British architecture "is stuck in the Modernist time-warp". The issue of London's modern architecture and its interaction with the past forms the basis of his talk, looking at how apparently failing areas such as the East End can become the heart of regeneration.

Organised and supported by Blueprint
Sponsored by Cundall, Pipers, Collyer Bristow, Kingston Smith, Austin-Smith: Lord

Jude Kelly

One of the most respected figures on the UK arts scene, Jude Kelly is art director at the South Bank Centre and chair of the Arts, Education and Culture Committee for the 2012 London Olympics. She discusses her development plans for the South Bank Centre, and how they are influenced by the 1951 Festival of Britain.

Boris Johnson

The former editor of *The Spectator*, current MP for Henley on Thames and cycling enthusiast has expressed strong opinions on the current government's culture politics and the handling of the arts in Britain. For the breakfast he applies his unique critical faculties to London's built environment.

Location
Smiths of Smithfield
Charterhouse Street
London EC1M

The sacred river
Talk by Peter Ackroyd

*Supported by
Tate Modern*

"In the Neolithic period, the Thames was the principal centre of spiritual activity. There are five causewayed enclosures by the river; there are also twelve chambered long barrows, eight earthern long barrows, five smaller barrows and two henge monuments. They seem to have been chosen for that particular vantage, and no other, close to the waters. They are generally on the site of previous Mesolithic activity, too, which suggests that the same riverine locations had been in employment for many thousands of years. There are cursus monuments and henge monuments directly related to the flow and current of the river. Ritual deposits and votive offerings have been left in it since the period of the Upper Palaeolithic.

"The holy traditions of the Thames have been continued for the past 2,000 years. Votive offerings from the Celtic, Roman and Saxon peoples have been found in great quantities along certain stretches. Heads were thrown into the waters as a form of human sacrifice. The Christian faith also took over the worship of the waterway. It is a river of churches. In particular, there are no fewer than 50 churches, chapels and chantries devoted to the Virgin Mary along its banks. This would seem to be related to the fact that it is also the home of the "Mother Goddess" of Celtic veneration. Which is also why the Thames in its upper reaches is still sometimes known as the Isis, in honour of the Mother Goddess of Egyptian worship. It is still a sacred river."

Location
Tate Modern
Bankside
London SE1 9TG

Neo-utopia (imaginative future city)
Lecture by Kumiko Shimizu

Supported by London Borough of Camden and Space Shift

"Recent disasters such as the tsunami in south-east Asia and Hurricane Katrina in America have made us more aware of issues concerning the environment. Climate change, pollution, migration and urban design are questioned in order to bring about a reassessment of what is going on with current policies and activities.

"As an artist/urban designer, my primary endeavour is to interrogate the relationship between man and nature. Urbanism is what I have been questioning and experiencing through my art activities. My approach to the future city is not only structured in terms of survival, but how man can be content and happy with his existence. Urban design is not just allocating buildings and transportation systems, but requires a deep comprehension of man and his dwelling. This consequentially demands a knowledge of philosophy, science, technology and community orientation. Sustainability is among the most talked about subjects within urbanism. Renewable energy, speedy communication systems and developments of technology could contribute to our lives

and bring us nearer to the natural world from which we originally came. After consideration of all these aspects, I created the future city as a co-habitation of man and nature. In my city, animals take on a significant role as indicators of the likelihood of man's survival.

"My idea for the future city is a development where humans live in a vertical dimension and animals live on the ground in the horizontal dimension. Ideally, all animals will be left alone and will not be interfered with by humans. The city will be sustainable as a result of renewable energy generated by solar power and wind. Water will be collected from rain and the atmosphere, and all sewage and human waste will be used as a renewable fertiliser. This city is just a metaphor. In reality, animals, especially domestic animals, could live within the urban set-up, not necessarily in a city farm, but integrated into the human habitat.

"We live in a space artificially created by man, not by God, as punishment for having eaten a forbidden apple."

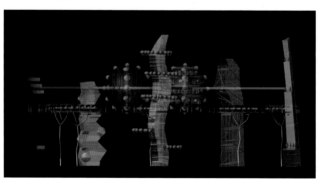 

Above and right:
Project for a site in
Death Valley California
by Kumiko Shimizu

Location
Space Shift
Cromer Street
London WC1H 8BZ

120

Change channel
Talk by Robert Elms

Organised by
Pollard Thomas
Edwards Architects

The writer, broadcaster, London enthusiast and Architecture Week patron explores the history, mystery and allure of the capital's watery byways.

Between midday and 3pm each weekday Robert Elms presents a wide-ranging magazine show on BBC Radio London which regularly deals with architectural issues. The show includes guests from the arts, entertainment, media and politics, as well as features on linguistics, design, film, music and food and drink from regular contributors. Maxwell Hutchinson and Austin Williams contribute on architecture.

Robert is London born and bred. He was educated at Orange Hill Grammar School, LSE and Queen's Park Rangers. He lives in a modernised Regency house in Camden and likes QPR, jazz and things that look good. He is a keen cyclist.

Location
Pollard Thomas
Edwards Architects
Diespeker Wharf
38 Graham Street
London N1 8JX

Meet the architecture editors

*Organised by
International
Building Press*

Top: Paul Finch. Above:
Eleanor Young. Right:
Jeremy Hunt. Below:
Vicky Richardson

This intensive two-hour seminar brings together eight leading editors in a format that enables delegates to put forward their views and questions on the way they work with the media. The session is particularly relevant to those responsible for media relations and communications issues, including professionals, contractors and communications managers, whether in-house or consultants.

The panel features: Paul Finch, editor, *Architectural Review*; Ian Latham, editor, *Architecture Today*; Jeremy Hunt, editor, *Art & Architecture*; Denise Chevin, editor, *Building*; Vicky Richardson, editor, *Blueprint*; Giles Barrie, editor, *Property Week*; Ruth Slavid, editor, *AJ Specification* and special features editor, *Architects' Journal*; and Eleanor Young, deputy editor, *RIBA Journal*. Each will commence with a brief statement on the editorial policy and focus of his or her magazine. The forum is chaired by Canon David Meara.

Location
St Bride's Church
Fleet Street
London EC4

Bring fronts back

*Organised by
GMW Architects*

*Supported by
Guardian
Newsroom*

Modest things can sometimes have a big impact on our lives. In many areas of London the streets are blighted because people seem to have lost interest in the space in front of their houses.

While CABE, the GLA and some London boroughs work hard to improve the public realm, it seems that this important private area has become a great lost cause. Though it can happen anywhere, the effect seems most acute in areas of low to medium value terraced and semidetached houses. As long as there is enough room to get one or two cars off the road, homeowners tend to turn their back on the front and consequently often-brutal adaptations to accommodate cars and rubbish bins set the tone. The result is the virtual abandonment of pride and expression in the front garden.

Such widespread erosion of the quality of life warrants a search for affordable remedies that are easily implemented. Terry Brown and colleagues from GMW Architects have started a campaign to try to reverse this tide, with a number of activities and ideas that can be viewed at www.bringfrontsback.com. Brown explains: "The aim is to set up an ideas network for things that can be done to recover pride and enjoyment in our residential fronts-of-house. This is not a witch-hunt. We do not propose to be arbiters of taste. We will ask questions. We will present examples of the good, the bad and the ugly. We will aim to be catalytic in generating ideas. But we ask you to make the judgments, and we ask you to think again about your front door."

At the London Architecture Biennale the GMW team presents the arguments in a rallying experience, talk and discussion.

Location
Newsroom, Guardian
and Observer Archive
and Visitor Centre
60 Farringdon Road
London EC1R 3GA

Architecture for Humanity (UK)

Supported by BDP

Architecture for Humanity (UK) (AfH UK) is a not-for-profit organisation concerned with the built environment. It seeks to bring together the expertise of individuals, professionals, organisations, groups and agencies to deliver quality solutions in architecture, planning and the built environment to help communities in need and organisations working for charitable causes.

The AfH UK Lecture Series, consisting of one lecture a month with a concluding symposium in October, covers topics relating to humanitarian work, such as design, the design process, building technology and politics. Design academics, practitioners, students and other organisations involved in humanitarian work share experiences and learn about design endeavours around the world and how the design profession is responding differently to human needs.

Top and above:
Architecture for
Humanity (UK) has
provided emergency
housing for projects in
crisis areas all over the
world

Location
The Presentation Room
BDP
Brewhouse Yard
London EC1V 4LJ

Euston Road: a place not a through road
Talk by Sir Terry Farrell

Organised by
London Borough
of Camden
Supported by
London &
Continental
Railways

"It's part of the job of the urbanist to make propositions. For this lecture, I'm going to look at our proposals for the Marylebone-Euston Road – one of London's greatest assets – and how they affect the public realm. As a long-term resident, I am fascinated by the huge potential for improvement of what is arguably London's best-connected street. From as early as 2002, we have produced a series of studies and proposals focusing on reinforcing the idea of the Marylebone-Euston Road as a place, not a through road. These are now gaining momentum.

"There is extraordinary growth happening along the road with major projects – King's Cross at one end, Paddington Basin at the other, air rights over Euston and the Regent's Place development on which we are working with British Land. There are great opportunities to connect pedestrian routes and the parks, and our proposals for the Nash Ramblas are progressing well.

"Also of significance is our detailed design study for the Marylebone-Euston Road underpass, which aims to create a pedestrian-friendly connection between Fitzrovia and areas to the north by retaining the underpass, but simplifying traffic and pedestrian movement and creating an enlarged new London square.

"This event gives an opportunity for a discussion on how we might imaginatively improve the Marylebone-Euston Road and celebrate urban life in this strategically important area."

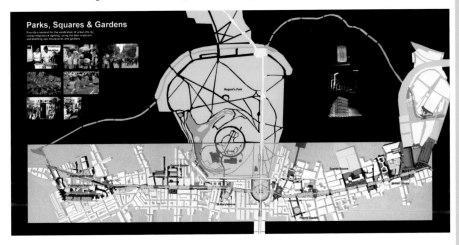

Terry Farrell's vision of a
revitalised Euston Road

Location
The Gymnasium
Pancras Road
London NW1 2TB

Richard Wentworth lecture

*Organised by
London Borough
of Camden
Supported by
Space Shift*

Richard Wentworth is an artist who has
known the King's Cross area for 40 years.
In this lecture he discusses whether
the people who live in the city own it,
or whether perhaps they are owned by
the city itself.

Above: Greetings from
King's Cross – an
Edwardian postcard,
c.1909

Location
Space Shift
Cromer Street
London WC1H 8BZ

Architectural design and urban change – the role of civic leadership

Organised by London Borough of Camden

A chaired discussion and debate on the role of local authorities in enabling high-quality development encompasses areas including Euston Road and King's Cross.

The London Borough of Camden is currently working with architects and developers across a number of schemes that aspire to provide the highest quality in design of the public realm. In today's economic and regulatory climate, where there are huge demands on public funds and high public expectations, how does a local authority successfully deliver excellence? How does it provide leadership in planning while listening to the community, when Londoners, visitors and local residents use many of our sites?

Location
Camden Town Hall
extension
Argyle Street
London WC1H 8EQ

1960s architecture: iconic or eyesore?

*Organised by
Southwark
Council with
BBC Radio 3
Night Waves*
*Supported by
Tate Modern*

Are 1960s buildings an eyesore or an icon of
their generation? Key figures in design and
architecture argue the case for and against
1960s design in a debate broadcast by BBC
Radio 3 on *Night Waves*.

Location
Tate Modern
Bankside
London SE1 9TG

The Brunswick Centre
Lecture by Patrick Hodgkinson

*Organised by
London Borough
of Camden*
*Supported by
The British Library*

The Brunswick Centre is an iconic example
of late 1960s architecture and urban design.
It is currently nearing the end of a renovation
programme, begun in 2004, and will soon
re-emerge painted cream – bringing it nearer
to the original vision of the architect Patrick
Hodgkinson, which he talks about here.

Situated between King's Cross and
Russell Square, the centre provides a diverse
residential community housed in both
privately owned and council flats.
Pedestrian-only terraces give access
to shops, a supermarket and the Renoir
Cinema. Like many visionary developments,
it has attracted both praise and criticism.
What is without doubt is the dramatic
impact it has had on the streets of
Bloomsbury.

Location
The British Library
Conference Centre
Euston Road
London NW1 2DB

Reinventing the Bike Shed

Run by Blueprint in collaboration with the Design Against Crime Research Centre, Feilden Clegg Bradley Architects and Southwark Cyclists

Location
Tooley Street Arches
access via On Your Bike
The Arches
52–54 Tooley Street
London Bridge
London SE1 2SZ

This public seminar, organised by Feilden Clegg Bradley, *Blueprint* magazine, Southwark Cyclists, Design Against Crime Research Centre and Sogol Architects, launches the *Blueprint* "ideas" competition, Reinventing the Bike Shed, which is looking for new solutions to inner-city bike storage in public spaces, workplaces and the home, on any scale and for any end use – from a one-off locking device in your backyard to a large-scale bike shed – within two categories. The seminar includes contributions from *Blueprint*, bike theft researchers, designers, architects and planners. The aim is two-fold: to find practical proposals which could go into production and to push the boundaries by floating extreme or eccentric ideas that challenge current thinking. It is organised in conjunction with CABE.

The Big Crit

Organised by Pippa Gueterbock, EDAW
Supported by Guardian Newsroom, London Metropolitan University, archaos, Ove Arup Foundation, Fluid, The Happold Trust

Location
Guardian Newsroom
Archive and Visitor
Centre
60 Farringdon Road
London EC1R 3GA

Students present their interventions for discussion with a panel of architects and the public. Here are just two examples:

Central Saint Martins College of Art and Design (MA Narrative Environments): Story Bubble
A wayfinding project touched with fantasy: an oversized bubblegum machine in Smithfield Market contains messages on the gumball papers, written by school children, which suggest little events and tell little stories (or little fantastical lies) about the place's history.

London Metropolitan University, Department of Architecture and Interior Design: 140 Boomerangs
The spiralling roadway in West Smithfield is echoed by a helix tower placed in the central garden, drawing attention to one of London's hidden architectural gems and the biennale. A local children's clay sculpture exhibition is held in the bumpy interior of the timber structure, which wraps the "peace" fountain at the centre.

Regeneration: what are the successful ingredients?

Organised by
Southwark
Council
Supported by Tate
Modern

Delving into the complex issues surrounding the regeneration of our ageing capital, leading figures from the world of architecture and urban planning ask what it takes to create a sustainable London, and how to spend regeneration funds wisely.

A *Question Time*-style debate involves architect Will Alsop, Southwark Council's Chris Horn, urban violence expert Sophie Body–Gendrot, Borough Market's George Nicholson, Architecture Foundation Director Rowan Moore and Tate Modern's Vivienne Bennett, with Ricky Burdett, Centennial Professor in Architecture and Urbanism at the LSE and a member of the Greater London Authorities Architecture and Urbanism Unit, as the chair.

Above: Tate Modern

Location
Tate Modern
Bankside
London SE1 9TG

Creating the future – the creative and cultural industries in King's Cross St Pancras

Organised by
London Borough
of Camden
Sponsored
by London
Communications
Agency

King's Cross, traditionally an area of diversity, is undergoing great change. An invited panel looks at how King's Cross is to grow as a hub for the creative industries. Panel members include Roger Madelin (Argent) and Sir Michael Bichard (University of the Arts London). The event is sponsored by London Communications Agency.

Location
The Gymnasium
Pancras Road
London NW1 2TB

Twentieth Century Society walks

*Organised by the
Twentieth Century
Society*

1. Clerkenwell to King's Cross (northern route) The theme of this walk is twentieth-century buildings along the biennale route. Starting at Farringdon Underground Station in Cowcross Street, it goes via St John's Gate, Clerkenwell Green, St John Street, the Finsbury Health Centre, Exmouth Street and Gray's Inn Road to finish at King's Cross Underground.

2. Southwark to Clerkenwell (southern route) A second twentieth-century buildings walk goes from Tate Modern across the Millennium Bridge to St Paul's, Patternoster Square, Cheapside, Gresham Street, Aldersgate Street, the Barbican, Golden Lane and Smithfield, to Cowcross Street, finishing at Farringdon Underground.

3. Bankside A twentieth-century architecture themed walk along the south bank of the Thames starts at Tate Modern and finishes at London Bridge Underground. It looks at pre-war and post-war developments on both sides of the river and the new projects about to start on the north bank between Southwark and London Bridges.

4. Golden Lane Two walks around this seminal post-war social housing scheme, led by local residents Roland Jeffery and Paul Lincoln, allow access to some flats.

The Twentieth Century Society, founded as the Thirties Society in 1979, is the national amenity society that fights to safeguard the best of architecture and design in Britain from 1914 onwards. It campaigns for all styles of twentieth-century architecture and for all types of building – from phone boxes to factories.

The society receives a small grant from English Heritage, but the majority of funding comes from membership subscriptions and donations. Members and supporters include many eminent architects and designers, but most are just enthusiasts. Membership benefits include:

● Newsletter published three times a year, packed with news and background information.

● Members-only tours and walks – many giving access to buildings that are otherwise inaccessible.

● Overseas trips – with privileged access to local sites and expertise.

● Email updates on current campaigns.

● Lectures by acknowledged experts.

● Illustrated journal with in-depth essays by architects and historians.

● Access to 25 years' worth of notes to guided tours.

● The knowledge that you have helped to save important architectural works for future generations.

www.C20society.org.uk

Location
Farringdon
Underground Station
Tate Modern
Tate Modern
Golden Lane

Barbican flat tours

Organised by
Frank Harris

Our tour takes in a selection of the Barbican apartments. Built between 1956 and 1981 to designs by the private practice of Chamberlin, Powell & Bon, the Barbican development was Grade II listed in 2001. There are a total of 2,014 apartments with 127 styles. All its buildings are named after people who in the main had an association with the City of London or lived locally.

Andrewes House Lancelot Andrewes (1555–1626) – theologian, famous preacher, Vicar of St Giles for seventeen years. Eventually Bishop of Winchester.

Ben Jonson House Ben Jonson (1572–1637) – actor, playwright, (*Bartholomew Fair*, etc). Lived for some years in the parish of Cripplegate.

Brandon Mews Robert Brandon (fourteenth century) – Earl of Suffolk. Granted the Manor of Basecourt (known as Barbican) by Edward III in 1336.

Breton House W Bryer and Sons (nineteenth–twentieth century) – gold and silver refiners, watchmakers, etc. Premises in Barbican Street.

Bunyan Court John Bunyan (1628–1688) – preacher, author of *The Pilgrim's Progress*. Preached in Monkwell Street, buried in Bunhill Fields.

Cromwell Tower Oliver Cromwell (1599–1658) – soldier, statesman, Lord Protector of the Commonwealth. Married Elizabeth Bourchier at St Giles' Church.

Defoe House Daniel Defoe (1660–1731) – journalist, author of *Robinson Crusoe*, etc. Probably born in Fore Street. Died in Ropemaker Street and buried in Bunhill Fields.

Frobisher Crescent Sir Martin Frobisher (1535–1534) – sailor. Knighted during the Battle of the Armada. Buried St Giles' Cripplegate.

Gilbert House Sir Humphrey Gilbert (1539–1583) – explorer, soldier, sailor. Drowned off the Azores following successful expedition to Newfoundland. Lived at one time in Redcross Street.

John Trundle Court John Trundle (c.1600) –

Location
Frank Harris & Company
87 Long Lane
London EC1A 9ET

stationer. Premises in the Barbican. Published, with Nicholas Ling, the first quarto of William Shakespeare's *Hamlet*.

Lambert Jones Mews Richard Lambert Jones (b.1783) – member of the Court of Common Council for the ward of Cripplegate Without. Chairman of Library Committee for nineteen years.

Lauderdale Tower John Maitland (1616–1682) – created first Earl of Lauderdale by Charles I in 1624. One of his homes was Lauderdale House on Aldersgate Street.

Milton Court John Milton (1608–1674) – poet, author of *Paradise Lost* (1667) and *Paradise Regained* (1671). Lived for some time in Barbican area. Buried St Giles' Cripplegate.

Mountjoy House Christopher Mountjoy – Huguenot refugee who came to London in 1572. Made women's hats and lived in Silver Street.

Seddon House George Seddon (d.1801) – master cabinet maker. Established huge furniture emporium in Aldersgate Street.

Shakespeare Tower William Shakespeare (1564–1616) – actor, poet, playwright. Born in Stratford-upon-Avon but spent most of his working life in London. Known to have lodged at the Mountjoys in Silver Street in 1604.

Speed House John Speed (1522–1629) – merchant tailor, historian and cartographer. Produced a series of maps of the countries of England and Wales. Buried St Giles' Cripplegate.

Thomas More House Sir Thomas More (1478–1535) – statesman, author, lawyer. Imprisoned in the Tower of London and eventually beheaded. Born in Cripplegate Parish.

Willoughby House Catharine Willoughby, Duchess of Suffolk (1520–1580) – upholder of the new "Protestant beliefs". Taunted Bishop Gardiner and later forced to flee abroad temporarily from her home in the Barbican.

Shakespeare, social space and design:
The Globe and Royal Shakespeare Theatre

WALKS & TOURS

Organised by Southwark Council in association with David Marshall and Rab Bennetts
Supported by The Globe

David Marshall leads an informal journey through Elizabethan Bankside, from the George Inn and the site of the Rose Theatre to the reconstructed Globe. It takes an irreverent look at the happy accidents which led to the first purpose-built public theatres and finds out what secrets they might hold for us today.

Also, Rab Bennetts presents his firm's design for the new Royal Shakespeare Theatre in Stratford-upon-Avon, the planning application for which is due to be lodged shortly. The scheme takes a broad view of the theatre and its context, with masterplanning ideas that embrace a new public square, connections to nearby buildings and routes along the riverside and beyond. The main performance space itself is in thrust format, with a wholly new auditorium inserted within the existing art deco building.

Rab's talk outlines the influences on the design and its response to current thinking about the performance of Shakespeare, with reference to the historic context outlined by David Marshall.

Right: site of the Rose Theatre. Below and far right: the reconstructed Globe

Location
The George Inn
Borough High Street
London SE1 9DA

King's Cross Voices presents the Argyle Square Sound Trail

Organised by King's Cross Community Development Trust

Supported by Heritage Lottery Fund, London Borough of Camden, London Borough of Islington, Argent and The British Library

King's Cross is in the throes of a massive transformation triggered by the redevelopment of the former railway lands and the arrival of the Channel Tunnel link in 2007. Dominated by King's Cross and St Pancras Stations, the area has always been much more than just a point of arrival and departure.

The King's Cross Oral History Project was set up in 2004 by the King's Cross Community Development Trust to record people's stories of their life and work in the area. Run by a team of two full-time staff and a host of enthusiastic volunteers, King's Cross Voices is planning to interview some 300 people documenting the remarkable range of communities and occupations, both past and present, which make up the tapestry of this unique district of London.

Compiled from King's Cross Voices interviews, the Argyle Square Sound Trail takes the listener on a voyage of discovery around one of the area's most residential and least documented historic quarters. Participants, armed with an illustrated booklet that accompanies the trail, follow a sign-posted route weaving in and around the adjoining side streets before settling in Argyle Square.

The square overlooks the iconic terminae of King's Cross and St Pancras. Today, it's best known for its hotels, for having one of the very few green spaces in the locality, as a key location in the 1955 Ealing Comedy classic *The Ladykillers* and, until recently, for its rather seedy reputation.

It was built in the 1830s, when the district was still known as Battle Bridge, on the projected site of the Royal London Panaramonion – a wondrous flop of a scheme that imagined a botanical bazaar, a suspension railway, a music academy and art galleries set in ornate pleasure gardens. Instead, Argyle Square, with its houses with round-arched doorways, became home to the middle classes, artists and professionals. By the turn of the twentieth century it slowly began to give way to the lure of hotels to house visitors pouring out of the great stations.

The Argyle Square Sound Trail, lasting about 30 minutes, is accessible throughout the LAB week either by downloading it from the King's Cross Voices website, www.kingscrossvoices.org.uk, or by loan on CD (CD player also available, if needed) from the St Pancras Library in Argyle Street, or the German Gymnasium on Pancras Road.

Right: a vision from Argyle Square's past

Location
www.kingscross
voices.org.uk

Change channel watery journeys

*Organised by
Pollard Thomas
Edwards Architects
in association with
All Change Arts,
the Islington Boat
Club and Hanover
Primary School
Supported by
Mediashore Ltd*

Through the watery mist and sound of a thudding heartbeat, the tunnel entrance approaches. As the darkness envelopes the vessel, fragments of children's voices tell of the myths associated with this forgotten London artery. The bubbling engine suddenly stops and the boat begins to glide in the blackness to the echoing of navvies' feet, who once pushed against the tunnel walls on their backs to propel the boats through. Somewhere in the cold distance a light begins to dance on the water's surface…

Visitors travel on a "choreographed" journey by bell boat through the Islington Regent's Canal tunnel between the King's Cross Regent Quarter Development and City Road Lock, the location of the offices of Pollard Thomas Edwards Architects (PTEa).

Together with our sponsor partners Mediashore Ltd and collaborators from City Road Basin, including All Change Arts, The Islington Boat Club and Hanover Primary School, a series of workshops have been initiated to explore the myths and characters associated with the tunnel. Working with artist Carl Stevenson, children have conceived new characters and stories to develop a collection of signs, costumes and soundscapes as inspiration for his installation within the tunnel.

The installation continues into the garden and meeting spaces of PTEa's office at Diespeker Wharf, where visitors can enjoy refreshments and an exhibition. Diespeker acts as an intermediate location along the biennale route, linking the key nodes of King's Cross and nearby Smithfield Market.

Right: the Pollard
Thomas Edwards office
in King's Cross. Overleaf:
Pollard Thomas Edwards
is choreographing a trip
through the Islington
Regent's Canal tunnel

Location
Pollard Thomas
Edwards, Diespeker
Wharf, 38 Graham
Street, N1 8JX
and London
Canal Museum
12 New Wharf Road
London N1 9RT

Siobhan Davies Studios: dance and architecture under the ribbon roof

Organised by Siobhan Davies Studios and Southwark Council

This tour of the Siobhan Davies Dance Studios has been organised by the London Borough of Southwark.

The new studios are the result of a close collaboration between the choreographer Siobhan Davies and architect Sarah Wigglesworth (Sarah Wigglesworth Architects, www.swarch.co.uk), involving the major refurbishment and extension of a redundant three-story building, dating from 1898 and located in the playground of the Charlotte Sharman Foundation Primary School in St George's Road, Southwark. A bold, organic design breathes new life into the old structure, enhancing it with contemporary elements such as an impressive two-storey atrium and a signature undulating roof in the main performance space.

Following the tour, Siobhan Davies and Sarah Wigglesworth discuss their work together on this project and the dance piece *In Plain Clothes*, which opened the building in April. They are also joined by dancer/choreographer Carol Brown and architect Mette Ramsgard Thomsen, who talks about their collaboration on an architecture-based dance performance/installation, *Sea, Unsea*.

Right: Siobhan Davies Dance Studios by Sarah Wigglesworth Architects

Location
Siobhan Davies Studios
85 St George's Road
London SE1 6ER`

Passeggiata – a ritual promenade

*Organised by Julia
Wright, Squire and
Partners and
Giorgia Mancini*
Sponsored by
Squire and
Partners and
Fulcrum
Consulting Ltd

The Passeggiata combines two of the
capital's great passions – architecture and
food. Participants walk the biennale route
from Borough Market through the City and
Clerkenwell to King's Cross, pausing along
the way to look, listen, eat and drink.
Temporary installations and exhibitions are
dotted along the way, and groups are led by
architectural commentators who provide
information about buildings and sights.

To start off the day, a breakfast of freshly
ground coffee and pastries is served in
Winchester Square, just behind Borough
Market, from three-wheeler Piaggio vans
supplied by Caffé Mobile. From here the walk
takes in the South Bank, the Millennium
Bridge, Paternoster Square and the City
of London, before arriving at the next food
stop, the historic meat trading grounds
of Smithfield Market.

Lunch is a spectacular Italian feast
comprising a freshly carved porchetta
(whole roasted pig) with accompanying
salads and pagnotta bread, served at tables
under the arches of the Grand Avenue of
Smithfield Market, a fine example of
Victorian market design. The group then
moves north to St John's Square for the
next course – a refreshing dessert of gelato
and sorbet, plus fresh Italian coffee,
provided by the Zetter Hotel and Restaurant
outside its premises overlooking the Order
of St John.

The walk continues to lively Exmouth
Market for a digestif prepared by Brindisa,
specialist importers of Spanish food and
drink, where participants can choose from
a tipple of Manzanilla or Fino sherry to wash
down a cigarillo biscuit or an almond torta.

Winding its way further north to King's
Cross, the group visits the Lloyd Baker
Estate, before calling in at 6 St Chad's Place
bar and restaurant, a striking warehouse
conversion on a King's Cross back street,
for a refreshing Pimm's or G&T to relax the
muscles after a hard day's eating.

Supported by
Southwark Council,
Borough Market, City
of London, Smithfield
Market, London
Borough of Islington,
The Zetter, Brindisa,
London Borough
of Camden and
6 St Chads Place

Above: Borough Market,
start of the Passeggiata

Location
Start at Winchester
Square
London SE1 9AP

Looking with your feet: beating the bounds of 21st-century Clerkenwell

*Organised by
Mike Franks
and John Bailey*

The Saxon chroniclers used written "maps" to describe areas. Medieval parish elders had boys "beaten" at boundary corners to reinforce generations of folk memory. Even in eighteenth-century Clerkenwell, boundaries were still walked. So this is what we are doing, but in historic rather than administrative Clerkenwell. Our purpose is to define the "commons", celebrate the public realm and "look with our feet" to learn what the sloping ground can tell us about the water themes that so influenced Clerkenwell's past. Our walk initiates the first year of the Clerkenwell Commons programme.

For almost 1,000 years, development in Clerkenwell has evolved slowly, resisting annexation by the City and retaining a creative spark that continues today. Significant water themes have influenced this evolution, two of which reach back to an inter-glacial period when the proto-Thames (then a tributary of the Rhine) laid down the well-drained gravel bed cut through by the River Fleet with springs of "sweet water" and deep aquifers that were to supply the Norman religious houses, Georgian pleasure gardens and Victorian gin makers.

We look at the two linked historic "squares" that are the centrepiece of our walk, and visit the Clerks' Well. Both spaces effectively became common land at the dissolution of the monasteries, and together they figure as a major urban set piece that has been neglected for decades. On the west

and east our boundaries trace the line of the River Fleet and an ancient drovers' track. Smithfield marks the south and the glacial slope before Sadler's Wells the north. Administrative Clerkenwell is both wider and longer, but our focus is land influenced by St Mary's Nunnery and St John's Priory, and their immediate medieval street patterns that have survived as backwaters because of the ruthlessness of the Victorian improvers.

Before it was "discovered", Clerkenwell hid for centuries behind the barrier of the Fleet, and as London grew it became overcrowded and profoundly unhealthy. Living with three prisons, a fetid river, a cattle drive and an abattoir, its people produced world-renowned clocks and instruments. From the 1870s, waves of slum clearances disrupted some lives and improved others. At the heart of this world city the tense interdependence between the formalised institutional core and the mixture of small-scale, informal, often non-conforming activity on the periphery has been the constant friction that produces the pearl, and Clerkenwell's relationship to the City comes as close as anywhere to being the creative, if uncomfortable, irritant that makes London healthy.

Here was the start of the East End: a district "beyond the Pale" that became one of the City's most unruly neighbours. The Commons programme seeks to recover mere spaces so they can again become meaningful places.

Right: Clerkenwell Common

Location
Clerkenwell Commons
26 Clerkenwell Close
London EC1R 0AG

London inclusive! Centre for Accessible Environments – Access Lab project

Organised by Adrian Cave, Centre for Accessible Environments Access Lab

The Centre for Accessible Environments (CAE) organises inclusive events and other projects in support of improving the built environment for all its diverse users. For the London Architecture Biennale there are two walks. One shows how far the capital has moved forward in becoming a publicly accessible city, designed around a step-free route from Tate Modern to the City. Architect and access consultant Adrian Cave talks about some of the best elements of historic and contemporary London. Here, accessibility and inclusion cease to be the main issue and the walk becomes more a time for discovering new things.

The other walk is from Sadler's Wells to Smithfield and also explores the sites/sights, both historic and contemporary. At the same time participants undertake a "live audit", discussing the highs and lows of the route's accessibility. Spray-on paint, disposable cameras, written questionnaires and voice recorders are used to record and share impressions. The resulting materials form part of an ongoing process of communicating issues around inclusive design more widely, and of making practical improvements to where we live and work.

Live audits are one of the many techniques used by CAE as a way of fostering genuine dialogue between informed users of the built environment and "deciders", such as planners, architects and interior designers. Put simply, this involves a group of people with different kinds of expertise, abilities and disabilities exploring a place together and reflecting jointly on their experiences. The process of mutual learning can identify surprising and often superior design responses that help us towards more inclusive environments. In developing this approach, CAE is now creating the Access Lab.

What is the Access Lab?

It will be a laboratory to explore the ideas and practicalities generated by the concept of inclusive design – a place where users and professionals can interact so as to improve awareness and understanding of accessibility and the built environment. The next stage is to use an existing "un-designed" 1,225 sq ft space to pilot some of the project's aims.

The Access Lab project believes that people are all different, but share aspirations – to participate in society and to belong. They do not need to be arbitrarily divided into able-bodied and disabled. There is no rulebook here or "right" solution for designers. It is not about separating people off as "special needs" or improving "disabled access" – it is about making buildings and landscapes which celebrate and support the realities of human diversity and difference.

CAE is an entrepreneurial charity, one of the leading authorities and resources in the UK on the practicalities of inclusive design in the built environment. It provides training, publications, consultancy and advice.

Location
Tate Modern
Bankside
London SE1 9TG

Upper Reaches,
Clerkenwell
London

Below and Above – archaeology and architecture tours

*Organised by
Kevin Flude*

Below and Above is a series of three tours taking in the Southwark, City and Smithfield/Clerkenwell areas. On each an archaeologist describes what was found below ground and an architect discusses the architecture above. The three districts have long and changing histories, and provide different models of successful change and redevelopment. The walks are conceived as a dialogue between archaeology and architecture; we hope to discover synergies between the past, present and future city.

Historic Southwark

Bankside is part of historic Southwark, which began as a series of islands surrounded by the Thames at high tide. The building of the first London Bridge transformed the area into a bridgehead settlement. With the Industrial Revolution, a mixed settlement of houses, hostelries and industry became one of world's major industrial and warehousing centres, whose buildings give Southwark its unique atmosphere today. In the 1980s it became an extension of the City. Then, with the building of the new Globe and Tate Modern, Bankside became a cultural quarter, and a new architectural landscape began to emerge.

City of London

The City of London developed on a "greenfield" site (c.47AD) immediately after the Romans built the first major bridge across the Thames. It soon became the most famous commercial centre in Britain and capital of the province. The Romans set the pattern for the City, whose citizens became rich on the back of trade and government. That pattern was changed in the nineteenth century when the port moved into the East End, and as business profits grew, the post-fire brick terraces were swept away by grandiose banks, trading floors and headquarters buildings. The City today is a showcase of formidable landmark architecture lining streets steeped in history.

Smithfield

Smithfield is an extramural settlement used by the Romans as a cemetery, and as a livestock market from the medieval period. The market space still dominates the area, surrounded by memorials of its use for public executions and by medieval monasteries. The former commercial and market buildings now house cultural industries, restaurants and nightclubs. An area once lively at night with porters and taxi drivers is now throbbing with clubbers.

Right: the City of London, a showcase of formidable landmark architecture

LAB bike tours – the changing face of London

Organised by Feilden Clegg Bradley and Southwark Cyclists in association with Bike Week and Sustainability Week

Supported by Blueprint, Aedas and Sogol Architects

Do you ride a bike? Do you want to find out more about the continuing evolution of London? Our architectural bike tours consider aspects of change within the capital, from the evolution of ideal living and lost schools, to new growth and regeneration. *Blueprint* magazine has produced illustrated maps outlining each route. Organised by Feilden Clegg Bradley and Southwark Cyclists, each ride is led by a specialist guide.

Urban change
Focusing on three streets from King's Cross, Smithfield and Bermondsey, we examine urban change at close quarters, considering London's highly developed system of layers and connections.

Changing rooms
Wayne Hemingway conducts a tour of iconic housing developments in inner London, charting how our architectural expectations have progressed since the nineteenth century.

Changing schools
Central London's schools are being extended and redeveloped at great speed. Many listed school buildings from the 1950s and 1960s may soon disappear, and this ride, both north and south of the river, shows the variety and quality of architecture that could be lost. The tour has been organised in conjunction with the Twentieth Century Society.

Midsummer's Day ride
Watch the sunrise from the top of Primrose Hill – the best time in the year to take in one of the best views of London, and well worth the early start. We begin at Cutty Sark Gardens, Greenwich, and end with breakfast at the Globe Theatre. The ride is led by Barry Mason of Southwark Cyclists.

Change and exchange
This is a tour of some of our best markets, from Borough to Billingsgate and beyond, to investigate how they have endured through the centuries and adapted to the changing needs of Londoners.

Water cycle
This tour takes in contemporary architecture along rivers and canals in central London.

Location
Tate Modern, front lawn
Bankside
London SE1 9TG

Iroko Housing Co-Op
(Coin Street Housing)
Upper Ground
London SE1 9PR

Main entrance,
The London College
of Communication
Elephant and Castle
London SE1 6SB

Cutty Sark Gardens
Greenwich
London SE10 9HT

The New Market
Smithfields pub
26 Smithfield Street
London EC1A 9LB

Princess Diana
Memorial
Serpentine Bridge
Hyde Park
London SW7

New and old around Bankside and Bermondsey

Organised by Southwark Council and Kenneth Powell

Supported by Allies and Morrison

Led by Kenneth Powell, author of *New London Architecture* (Merrell) and other books on the capital's architecture, this walking tour looks at more than twenty years of regeneration and redevelopment in Southwark. It takes in New Concordia Wharf, London's first large-scale loft-style conversion, Piers Gough's adjacent China Wharf, the Butler's Wharf area, Norman Foster's MoreLondon and City Hall, the stunning new Unicorn Theatre (where its architect Keith Williams conducts a short tour), Borough Market, Clink Street and the Bankside 123 office development by Allies and Morrison. The event ends with a look at Allies and Morrison's own offices on Southwark Street, one of London's most impressive architectural studios.

Right: the Unicorn Theatre, designed by Keith Williams

Location
The Design Museum
Shad Thames
London SE1 2YD

The top markets Route master tour

Organised by
Southwark
Council and SAVE
Supported
by St John
Restaurant

Markets are the very reason for the existence of many towns across the UK. In London they serve a variety of purposes, from tourism to retail, and are always busy centres of trade. This tour takes in a number of the most important market buildings in the capital, from King's Cross to Borough, via Covent Garden, Smithfield and Leadenhall. It includes appropriate refreshments on board, *en route* and at the final destination. Your compère for the evening is the incomparable Paul Finch, editor of *AR*, with expert commentary on the buildings from Roger Madelin, Jenny Freeman, Eric Reynolds and Ken Greig.

Location
The British Library
96 Euston Road
London NW1 2DB

15 Spaces – a unique perspective on the culture of public space in the City of London

Organised by
Space Syntax

As part of LAB06, Space Syntax is sharing its approach to the analysis and strategic design of the built environment by hosting a walk of the City of London. Originally conceived as an introduction to Space Syntax for postgraduate architecture students at University College London, it explores both well-known and hidden spaces in this unique urban area. Along the way, tour guides discuss and illustrate the fundamental links between the layout of the City – its "movement network" – and the way people navigate and experience its spaces, providing an insight into how Space Syntax theory works on the ground and how it can help us to understand the "spatial culture" of urban areas.

Location
11 Riverside Studios
28 Park Street
London SE1 9EQ

Barbitecture: architecture tours for families

Organised by the Barbican and Scarlet Projects

Look up, look down, look all around. An interactive walk explores the architecture of the Barbican. Keep the pace up and don't forget your walking shoes! Designed to give families new insights into the ideas behind the buildings and a chance to discover some of the hidden nooks and crannies. With design historian Sarah Gaventa of Scarlet Projects and artist Reza Ben Gajra. For children 7 and over.

Location
Barbican Art Gallery
Barbican Centre
Silk Street
London EC2Y 8DS

Borough Market experience

Organised by Southwark Council and Borough Market

Two tours of Borough Market, conducted by its chairman George Nicholson and architect Ken Greig from Greig + Stephenson Architects, explore the incredible journey of London's oldest market – from its ancient beginnings to the architectural story of its refurbishment and subsequent development as the flourishing fine food retail centre that Londoners and visitors know and love.

Location
Borough Market
8 Southwark Street
London SE1 1TL

Norman Foster: Building the Gherkin – UK premiere

Directed by
Mirjam von Arx
In association with
Barbican Cinema

A film season presented in association with the London Architecture Biennale complements the Barbican Gallery show 'Future City: Experiment and Utopia in Architecture 1956–2006'.

London is one of the world's leading film cities. It has played host to some major movies, and the city's architecture has been a key factor in the decisions of film-makers to locate their work in the capital. Through the lenses of the innovatively different film-makers in this programme, our concrete, steel and glass environments come to life and the city's mercurial identity is celebrated.

The films, *Building The Gherkin* and *Wheel*, are screened following an introduction by Norman Foster and a conversation between *Building The Gherkin*'s director Mirjam von Arx and architect and Gherkin project planner Carla Picardi.

Building the Gherkin

What can a single building do to the career of an architect, the image of a global company and the skyline of a big city? Just a month and a day after the 11 September attack, the first steel beam of a new skyscraper is erected in London. One question is on everybody's mind: is it the right decision to build an iconic tower in the midst of London's financial district, on a site that has already been bombed? The 40-storey steel and glass construction goes on to spark further controversy. Norman Foster, one of Britain's most visionary architects, calls his design for the new Swiss Re headquarters "radical… socially, technically, architecturally and spatially". In fact, its size and shape are so radical that it is immediately nicknamed "The Erotic Gherkin". Will the Gherkin become the landmark Foster and his team dream of?
Switzerland 2005, Dir. Mirjam von Arx. 89min.

Wheel

Following The London Eye from its blueprints, through the pods taking shape in a warehouse and the majestic arrival of sections down the Thames from the North Sea, this artistic work of minimal narrative and an eclectic soundtrack does justice to the new landmark.
UK 2000, Dir. Marcus Robinson, prod. Andrew Eaton, Michael Winterbottom and Gina Carter. 30min.

Location
Cinema 1
Barbican Centre
Silk Street
London EC2Y 8DS

Left and above: familiar
and unfamiliar views of
Foster Associates' Swiss
Re Building, better
known as the Gherkin.
Overleaf: the pinnacle of
the Gherkin under
construction

Social Cinema: a series of temporary cinemas

Neil Cummings
and Marysia
Lewandowska
With architects
Catherine du Toit
and Peter Thomas
51% Studios

Location
Social Cinema 1
Car Wash Wall
St John's Square,
London EC1
Social Cinema 2
Finsbury Health Centre
Pine Street
London EC1
Social Cinema 3
Paul's Walk under the
Millennium Bridge EC4

The Social Cinema project is a series of temporary cinemas with an improvisory architectural fabric – playful and subtle interventions into neglected space around landmark buildings are installed for one night only. In each place buildings become screens, steps seating, houses projection booths and unbuilt space auditoria. The Social Cinema traces a movement from the representation of everyday life to contemporary participation in those representations through mobile technologies.

Screened excerpts of lectures from the Architectural Association Photo and Film Library introduce ideas and observations by architects Cedric Price, Denys Lasdun, Reyner Banham, Jacques Herzog, Tom Heneghan and Ron Herron.

Above: Social Cinema 1. Tom Heneghan's *House for Raquel Welch*, video still from a lecture at the Art Net, London, 1976

Transit, a new film by Emily Richardson

Measurearts
with Emily
Richardson
Supported by Arts
Council England

The film is shown in the car park underneath Smithfield Market, at a juncture where the past encroaches upon the modern world. The recent two-storey car park carved up the former meat depot, leaving only one remaining row of the original full-height arched vaults.

Over the past year Emily has been researching the shifting architectural and social landscape of the east end of London, with the view to making a four-part short experimental, partially animated, 16mm film that captures something of the changes taking place. Measure has commissioned the first chapter for LAB06. It is an historical document, but a subjective and idiosyncratic one – a personal response to what is happening, informed by research and observations made in the area. Animated sections using camera techniques similar to those developed in Emily's past work, including time lapse, single frame and long exposure night shooting, are combined with bursts of "real time" tracking shots transporting the viewer from place to place within the film. Each shot or sequence is a description of a place, person, subject or object.

Measure is organising an evening screening of all Emily's films to date, introduced by the artist.

Location
Smithfield car park
London EC1

AA Social Cinema @ Scoop

Students: Bonnie Chu, Sarah Akigbogun, Jenny Kagan, Pavandeep S. Panesar, Carl Fraser. Mentors: Peter Thomas and Catherine du Toit of 51% Studios and David Crookes of Fluid Structures

Sponsored by MoreLondon, Camden Architects Forum/RIBA, BASE Structures, High End, Verseidag

The AA Social Cinema is a node in the main Social Cinema programme, though it differs in that MoreLondon offered the Architectural Association the use of the Scoop structure, a purpose-built sunken oval amphitheatre, clad in grey limestone, on The Queen's Walk, just west of City Hall. It is a new piece of formal public space on what was originally known as London's Larder, which then became the William Curtis Ecological Park until it was developed for the GLA.

Students from the AA, mentored by architects Peter Thomas and Catherine du Toit of 51% Studios and engineer David Crookes of Fluid Structures, bring the Scoop to life as an extension and reflection of the Thames by covering it with a horizontal billowing screen, upon which are projected moving images reflecting on the river as source, river as flow and river as change.

The aspects of change that relate to a river are multifarious. There is its own daily tide, which creates a rhythm, and there are the relatively slow changes that occur as a result of urban reorganisation and resulting architectural intervention. Within the environment created by these dual forces exist several layers of human activity, which will be explored with a series of short films from the AA archives, from commercial cinema and from students' own footage.

The Thames has an iconic presence within the city of London. To many it is a focal point and acts as a draw for the transient tourist population, but of what significance is it to Londoners? Often cast in a supporting role within the cinema, and occasionally as the main subject, the river's picturesque image appears repeatedly in films, from *Waterloo Bridge* in the 1940s through Hitchcock's *Frenzy* in the 1970s to the more recent manifestations. We are familiar with images of that massive body of tidal water with its statuesque bridges, such as Tower Bridge, but what exists beneath the celluloid surface? What does the film director's camera miss? Students are engaging in conversation with current users of the river and surrounding sites, the transient and the more permanent, in order to build a speculation about how the site might continue to evolve.

Thanks: Charlotte Bryant-Fenn, MoreLondon; David Crooks, Fluid Structures; Sam Collins and XL Video; Marion Marples (Community Liaison Officer), Southwark Cathedral; Nicholas Lacey, Tower Bridge Moorings; Joanna van der Meer, British Film Institute; Valerie Bennet and Henderson Downing, Architectural Association Photo Archive; Nicky Wynne, Architectural Association Development Office; Arup.

Right: a perspective of the AA Social Cinema @ Scoop

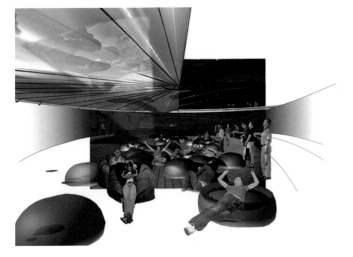

Location
Scoop
The Queen's Walk
London SE1 2AA

An audience with William Barlow (deceased)

FILM & TV

Written by Richard Shannon, directed by Peter Davies, produced by John Farquar-Smith
Sponsored by London & Continental Railways on behalf of the St Pancras Society

What was it like to build the great railway stations of the nineteenth century? How easy was the task compared with today? This is a unique opportunity to meet the famous engineer William Barlow, who in the nineteenth century created the great railway shed that in 2007 will welcome the latest Eurostar trains, and once was the finest building of its type in the world. He is brought back to life in a TV studio interview to give a modern audience an account of the struggle to build this cathedral of Victorian railway engineering. It was an epic achievement requiring 6,000 men, 1,000 horses and vast quantities of wrought iron. The railway crossed the Regent's Canal, pushed its way through the old St Pancras graveyard and obliterated the slum of Agar town. Barlow is also treated to a contemporary account of the restoration work now in progress.

Location
German Gymnasium
Pancras Road
London NW1 2TB

UK premiere of Lagos/Koolhaas

FILM & TV

Written and directed by Bregtje van der Haak
In association with Barbican Cinema

With a population of 14 million, Lagos is one of the fastest growing cities on the African continent and has a reputation for being one of the most dangerous in the world. For the past four years architect Rem Koolhaas and a team of students have regularly visited Nigeria's largest city to research the type of urbanity that is produced by uncontrolled, explosive population growth. Fascinated by the energy of Lagos, Koolhaas set out to learn from its structure and evolution, rather than planning, building or changing anything. *Netherlands 2002, Dir. Bregtje van der Haak, 55 min, In Nigerian, Dutch and English with English subtitles.*

Location
Cinema 3
Barbican Centre
Silk Street
London EC2Y 8DS

What have you done today, Mervyn Day?

*Directed by
Paul Kelly*
*Organised by
London Borough
of Camden
Supported by The
British Library*

Continuing the band Saint Etienne's deep-seated fascination with London and its inhabitants and buildings, *What Have You Done Today, Mervyn Day?* is set in the vast, mysterious pylon-covered wasteland that is the lower Lea Valley, east London, on the eve of the Olympic redevelopment. Through the eyes of a paperboy on his first day at work,

the band and film crew race against time to document buildings, landmarks and people before they disappear to make way for stadiums, spacious plazas and Olympic villages. With an accompanying musical score by Saint Etienne and narration by David Essex and Linda Robson.
UK 2005, Dir. Paul Kelly, 45 min.

Location
The British Library
Conference Centre
Euston Road
London NW1 2DB

Future City – London, Architecture and Film
The London Nobody Knows and Finisterre

*London Nobody
Knows directed by
Norman Cohen.
Finisterre directed
by Paul Kelly and
Kieran Evans*
*In association with
Barbican Cinema*

A film season presented in association with the London Architecture Biennale complements the Barbican Gallery show 'Future City: Experiment and Utopia in Architecture 1956–2006' (see page 152).

In a rare screening of a precious document that reveals the underside of London in 1967, James Mason acts as a guide to covert and esoteric parts of the city, showing us places which at that time had survived the bulldozer. *The London Nobody Knows* reveals the street markets, the homeless, the entertainers and the slums as it tours locations such as the Bedford Theatre, the men's toilets at Holborn Station and Chapel Market.
UK 1967, Dir. Norman Cohen, 53 min.

Also showing is *Finisterre* (PG), a hymn to London that takes us on a journey from the suburbs to the heart of the city, with a mesmerising score featuring the melancholy pop of Saint Etienne (Bob Stanley, Pete Wiggs and vocalist Sarah Cracknell). London has long been a source of influence, stimulation and curiosity for the band, and the film is a poignant "psycho-geographical" drama that celebrates the capital in both its seediness and glory. Exploring the dreams that it holds for so many alongside the reality of urban life, *Finisterre* was inspired by the James Mason-narrated 1967 gem, *The London Nobody Knows.*
UK 2003, Dir. Paul Kelly, Kieran Evans, 60 min.

Location
Cinema 1
Barbican Centre
Silk Street
London EC2Y 8DS

Sheep drive

EVENTS

*Organised by
Bennetts Associates
Architects and
Farmer Sharp*
Supported by
Bennetts Associates
Architects,
Southwark
Cathedral,
Borough Market,
Southwark
Council, City of
London, Smithfield
Market, Lord
Norman Foster

The sheep drive is one of the first events of the London Architectural Biennale 2006. It follows the great success of the cattle drive that opened the 2004 biennale, when six long-horned cows were paraded down St John Street. The 60 sheep are driven between the bustling Borough food market and the reinstated historic St Bartholomew's Fair.

The Herdwick animals are a pedigree breed introduced to England by Viking settlers in the tenth century. Farmer Sharp, who has a stall in Borough Market, brought them from their home on the hills of the Lake District, along with five sheep dogs and several shepherds. Two mounted police officers accompany the drive.

The journey starts in the courtyard of Southwark Cathedral, where they are symbolically sent on their way by the Bishop of Southwark. The flock is then led through Borough Market, along Clink Street and past the Globe Theatre and Sir Christopher Wren's house. Lord Foster joins them as they cross his Millennium Bridge, before they are driven up Peter's Hill past the new headquarters of the Salvation Army to the accompaniment of a brass band. The sheep pass in front of the west doors of St Paul's Cathedral, travel through Paternoster Square and then go on to the St Bartholomew Fair site at Smithfield. Here they are penned and rested for the day opposite the gateway to St Bartholomew's the Great, reputedly the oldest church in London.

Above: Farmer Sharp,
leader of the sheep drive

Location
Starts at Borough
Market
London SE1

St Bartholomew Fair

*Organised by ttsp
and Wilkinson
Eyre*
*Supported by ttsp,
Wilkinson Eyre,
City of London and
Smithfield Market*

Just as LAB04 focused around a lively street event, the opening Saturday of LAB06 has its own free public party. In 2004 more than 15,000 people crowded into St John Street to picnic, play, shop and watch the famous herd of cows retrace a historic route to Smithfield Market. This year, Smithfield is once again the hub of the biennale, hosting a re-creation of the ancient St Bartholomew Fair.

After greeting the sheep drive at Smithfield, the Sheriff of the City of London officially opens the day's activities, as was the tradition at the old event. As the animals spend the day in their own architect-designed pen in the shadows of St Bartholomew's Hospital, Smithfield Market and the surrounding streets, which are closed to traffic, are given over to the fair, organised as was the street party in 2004 by ttsp architecture + design.

Against a backdrop of market stalls selling a variety of goods, ranging from contemporary arts and crafts to mouth-watering food, there is a series of exciting cultural events, bringing alive the spirit of the old fair and evoking the richly layered history of this important public space. Highlights of the original St Bartholomew Fair, captured in Ben Jonson's famous play and Samuel Pepys's diaries, included acrobats, musicians, freak shows, jesters, theatrical performances and puppet shows. All these and more feature at the new fair – albeit with a contemporary, irreverent and architectural twist.

A focal point is an interactive megastructure – The Knitting Site. This amazing installation gradually unfolds throughout the day with the help of the public, quite literally spinning a yarn about Smithfield's history. It is complemented by smaller micro-installations around the area. Elsewhere, a promenade performance of Jonson's *Bartholomew Fair* takes place, while dancers and contemporary and traditional musicians mix with the crowds. Wandering players include "Oscar", local historian and self-confessed gossip, who whisks unsuspecting visitors on a unique architectural tour – focusing on what lies behind the walls.

There are demonstrations of traditional sparring and modern kick boxing, and a special area for children's activities. Wilkinson Eyre Architects, as well as curating the arts events, is running Secret Sketch, a sale of original (but anonymous) sketches by some of the world's leading architects, personalities and politicians. *News Pitch* pamphlets written and produced throughout the day give a real-time guide to what is happening.

The fair also provides an opportunity to view several of the biennale's most exciting other events and exhibitions. The 'Change' exhibition at the LAB06 HQ, Dallington School's paper bridge-building and a number of railing and student shows all take place in the vicinity of Smithfield – which itself lies at the centre of the 5km biennale route.

Fair organiser: Vanda Moyse, ttsp architects
Events curator: Emma Keyte, Wilkinson Eyre Architects
Knitting Site: Ana Araujo, Pooja Asher, Erica Calogero, Ana Matic, Jenny Wyness and Sagit Yakutiel
Micro-installation: Chik Kanamoto (Wilkinson Eyre Architects)
Human installation: Tom Geoghegan
Boxing demonstrations: Snipers Boxing Gym
Musicians include: Madarms, Experimental Music Project (Goldsmiths College)
Performers include: Phil Honour and Phil Nottingham (Central School of Speech and Drama)
News Pitch: Steve Austen-Brown (Pitch)
Secret Sketch: Emma Keyte and Damon Richardson (Wilkinson Eyre Architects)

Location
Smithfield Market
Charterhouse Street
London EC1A 9PQ

St Bartholomew Fair

Below: St Bartholomew
Fair 2006, as envisaged
by architects
Wilkinson Eyre

LONDON
ARCHITECTURE
BIENNALE
16-25 JUNE 2006
WWW.LONDONBIENNALE.ORG.UK

Architecture
Week

The Paper Bridge

Organised by Catherine du Toit and Peter Thomas of 51% Studios with Tim Macfarlane, Anderson Inge and Dallington School

"We are told never to cross a bridge until we come to it, but this world is owned by people who have 'crossed bridges' in their imagination far ahead of the crowd." – anon.

A collaboration between architects Peter Thomas and Catherine du Toit of 51% Studios, Tim Macfarlane of Dewhurst Macfarlane and Partners, Anderson Inge, an educator, engineer and sculptor, Fabian Hercules, a teacher and educational consultant, and children from years 5 and 6 at Dallington School has given birth to a six-metre paper suspension bridge.

The project focuses on the built environment and a "bridge" both as an object and as a linking device between two places – a suitable construction for a metropolis shaped by the Thames and the impact of the many bridges that cross it.

Using Clerkenwell's ties to the printing industry as inspiration, five cross-curricular workshops were designed to encourage the class to manipulate their physical surroundings; to take an idea from their imagination and make it support them and their classmates in real life.

The climax of the project is a bridge made from cheap and challenging materials that would not only hold the weight of the pupils, but also involve them in its construction. In fact, it only works if it is both built by them

and held in compression or tension by the children as the load.

This is the fourth year that we have made bridges with Dallington School for Architecture Week, and the second for the London Architecture Biennale. In 2004 we constructed a floating bridge from recycled water bottles to great effect in the courtyard of the Farmiloes Building.

Thanks: Friends of Dallington, www.friendsofdallington.co.uk; DuPont Tyvek®, www.tyvek.com; Essex Tube Windings Limited, www.essextubes.co.uk; Platipus Anchors Limited, www.platipus-anchors.com; Mogg Hercules, Dallington School; children, teachers and assistants at Dallington School, www.dallingtonschool.co.uk

Left, above and right: the paper bridge, designed and made by schoolchildren with the help of a team including engineers, architects and teachers

Location
St James Gardens
Sekforde Street
London EC1

Clerkenwell Green clean-up

Organised by
Matthew Lloyd
Architects, Price &
Myers and archaos
Supported by
London Borough
of Islington

As part of an ongoing debate about public spaces, we are cleaning and repairing some of Clerkenwell Green. The public can join in, and are welcome to talk to us as we work, exploring ideas about public and private, cleanliness and dirtiness, order and disorder, morality and ownership in relation to urban space. We are also joined by street artist Moose. Ben Campkin at the Bartlett School of Architecture, UCL, writes this about his work: "Through method and media, it confuses the categories of 'clean' and 'dirty' in an unsettling way... Moose's 'grime writing' begs the question: 'Who has the right to clean (or dirty) urban public spaces?' This prompts us to think about who owns and uses the urban environment, and who should be able to determine the boundary between private and public space." (To find out more about Moose's work, visit www.symbollix.com.)

Above: the work of street artist Moose "confuses the categories of 'clean' and 'dirty' in an unsettling way"

Right: Clerkenwell Green, in need of a clean-up

Location
Clerkenwell Green
London EC1

Future Farringdon

*Organised by
Richard Jones
(Jackson Coles),
Lee Mallet and AR
editor Paul Finch*

The area loosely known as Farringdon is now chiefly thought of as a through route, and as home to the busy Farringdon Underground station. The purpose of this project is to review Farringdon Road/Farringdon Street and their immediate environs, and to make propositions about their future.

Process

● Teams of architects, mainly local but some international, are each assigned a developer/property consultant to work as part of the team.

● Each team is invited to make an overall proposition about the area, and then focus on one particular area/activity within it.

● The day after the biennale opens, teams pin up/prepare presentations in a local exhibition venue.

● Presentation and discussion of the schemes takes place during the afternoon with a small invited panel chaired by Paul Finch.

● The pin-ups form an exhibition which remains in place for the duration of the biennale.

Right: Map of farringdon Road

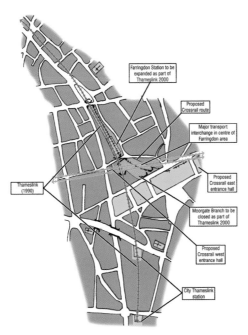

Location
Future Farringdon
Smithfield House
Charterhouse Street
London EC1

● The event and designs will be written up in a subsequent issue of *AR*.

The area

● *The London Encyclopedia* tells us that the area takes its name from a thirteenth-century goldsmith William de Farringdone, when Farringdon Street was created in 1737. This involved arching over the Fleet River.

● The Old Fleet Market was renamed Farringdon Market (fruit and vegetables) and comprised a large paved courtyard surrounded by shops. In the mid-nineteenth century it was well-known for sales of cress.

● The west side of the market was demolished when the approaches to the Holborn Viaduct were built in the 1860s, creating one of the few examples in London of a split-level city.

● Farringdon Road, an extension of Farringdon Street going north, was built in 1845, and was intended to cut through infamous slum areas. It stretches from Mount Pleasant, and followed the course of the Fleet River from Coldbath Fields Prison, through the Saffron Hill "rookeries" and on to Farringdon Street.

● The Metropolitan Railway was built parallel to the road, opening in 1863.

● Farringdon Station was once seen as the ideal station into which all mainline London trains would terminate, allowing passengers to switch lines at one central interchange.

● The station would play a key role in the proposed Crossrail route.

● Development over the Farringdon rail tracks has been much discussed, but cost of construction and height limits have inhibited activity.

● While there are distinct areas on either side of Farringdon Street/Farringdon Road, such as Smithfield and Hatton Garden, which do not form part of this event, there are others that could be more strongly identified as being part of Farringdon from an historical perspective.

The event is supported/organised by Richard Jones of Jackson Coles, development/communications consultant Lee Mallett and *AR* editor Paul Finch.

Ghosts of Borough Market: a magic lantern show in and about Borough Market

Christian Sievers
Hosted by General
Public Agency and
Ben Kelly Design

This performance lecture by artist Christian Sievers has been commissioned by General Public Agency and Ben Kelly Design, both long-term residents at Borough Market and witnesses to the changes the area has seen over the years.

Sievers's work explores unexpected and unlikely connections, here drawing upon the relationship between traders and customers, night and day, and neglected details of this particular forum of exchange.

In an interview with David Kulhanek in Prague in 2006, the artist says: "I like to think that the 'foundation' of my performances are the physical reality of things. The way one object relates to another. It starts with a certain image, say a pool of wine around a broken bottle on a supermarket floor, which then develops some kind of gravity and pulls in other images to complement it.

"The performance lectures are very much a hardened product, an artefact. It's then up to whoever cares to listen to retrace my steps, or to walk down a completely new path, in order to wrench some meaning from it. The fun of it is trying to match captions to images that have been dislocated – constructing a narrative out of heterogeneous elements that you suspect have something in common. But you don't know what it is. I myself sometimes have no idea; it makes new sense all the time.

If you like, the performance is in the head of the viewer.

"I use the slide form because everyone knows what to do at a lecture. I don't have to spend a lot of time establishing the framework. I'm taking a very formal way of presentation and using it for something else. Still, it's not improvised, and it doesn't have a casual feel to it. It's a bit pre-scientific, like magic lantern shows or anthropological lectures. Then, of course, I have to decide what I want this to be about, which questions to send out to people. That then triggers more images, and so on."

Sievers trained as a sculptor and performance artist, and has delivered performance lectures on a diverse array of subjects.

General Public Agency is a regeneration consultancy specialising in spatial, social and cultural analyses and strategies for the public realm.

An interior design practice, Ben Kelly Design was founded in the mid-1970s. It built its reputation producing high-profile and innovative spaces, including flagship fashion stores and Manchester's legendary nightclub the Haçienda. BKD has designed temporary, permanent and touring exhibitions, museum interiors, retail environments and headquarters offices for creative businesses and cultural institutions.

Left: Images from
Sievers' magic
lantern show

Location
Meet outside 10 Stoney
Street, Borough Market,
London SE1 9AD

Biennale Awards 2006

*In association
with New London
Architecture*
*Sponsored by
Pipers and Evening
Standard Homes
& Property*

Change is the London Architecture Biennale's overall theme this year, with the transformation of the architectural landscape of the city a major political and public talking point.

New buildings are springing up as part of major developments in King's Cross and Elephant and Castle, as well as for smaller private commissions all over the capital. The Biennale Awards 2006, sponsored by Pipers and the *Evening Standard Homes & Property*, asked architects and the public to submit, nominate and view projects online for the Best New Building Award and the London Hero Award via the New London Architecture website, www.newlondonarchitecture.org.

Online voting for the Best New Building opened on 20 May. Nominations could include buildings of any size or type completed in London since June 2004, be it a house or flat, a new restaurant, an office block, or a major skyscraper. Architects could also submit their recent projects, and the winner selected through online voting.

Politicians, architects, planners and directors of organisations have all had influence over the way the capital looks and works. The London Hero Award has been created to recognise the individual who has done the most in the past year to improve the quality of the environment in the city. All nominations were welcome, from politicians to celebrities, activists to general enthusiasts, and the winner selected by the London Architecture Biennale Committee.

The winners are announced by Nick McKeogh, director of Pipers, and Philippa Stockley, deputy editor of the *Evening Standard Homes & Property*, at St Bartholomew Fair.

Location
St Bartholomew Fair
Smithfield Market
Charterhouse Street
London EC1A 9PQ

Architecture, Art and Design Show 2006

Organised by
Midland Grand
Projects
Supported by
London Borough of
Camden and The
British Library

Right: work by one
of more than 50
contemporary artists
at the show

Midland Grand Projects is a non-profit organisation that develops unconventional and challenging formats for presenting visual art, encompassing environment and display. Passionate about architecture and environment, we have used this forum to open up normally inaccessible historical buildings such as St Pancras Chambers, Farmiloes of St John Street and Mary Ward House. For the London Architecture Biennale we are hosting the Architecture, Art and Design Show in the piazza of the British Library.

The London Art and Design Show launched in 2001. The venue for the first four events was the splendid and dramatic St Pancras Chambers, the former Midland Grand Hotel. This romantically derelict neo-Gothic building provided a theatrical setting that complemented installations of contemporary applied and fine art, and its notoriety brought in an initial large audience. The show then grew in reputation, becoming established enough to be mounted in other venues once the building was no longer available.

In 2004 it moved to the Farmiloes building on St John Street, site of the first London Architecture Biennale. The purpose-built late nineteenth-century warehouse complex sits majestically and discretely at the Smithfield end of the historic street. The exhibition made use of the many varied spaces in this vast venue. From wooden panelled Victorian offices to the four-storey glass covered atrium, Farmiloes provided an atmospheric derelict department store setting.

The following year saw us in Mary Ward House, reputed to be one of the finest examples of late nineteenth-century Arts and Crafts architecture. Working closely with the owners of the building, the show brought to life two floors of this exquisite venue. Artists displayed their work in the period ground-floor rooms, while the basement (including a double-height gymnasium) became a labyrinth of installations and gallery spaces.

For LAB06 our setting is of a very different nature, being a modern, specifically designed and well-used space. Our aim has been to create a ground-breaking and dynamic summer show by extending the use of the piazza at the British Library into a dramatic venue for art. Works by more than 50 contemporary artists are housed in inflatable white pavilions, while dance and performance events occur throughout the site.

Location
British Library Piazza
Euston Road
London NW1 2DB

The world's biggest Pecha Kucha

Idearight Klein Dytham. Organised by icon, ICA and Max Fraser
Sponsored by Bentley and Vitra in association with Sadler's Wells

Pecha Kucha is the networking and showcasing event that is taking the world by storm, and with an audience of up to 1,500, this is the largest ever staged. *ICON* magazine, Max Fraser and the London Architecture Biennale, with sponsors Bentley and Vitra, have come together to stage the one-off event to continue the legacy of the successful Pecha Kucha evenings held bi-monthly in conjunction with The Club at the ICA. Leading speakers from the worlds of architecture and design include Thomas Heatherwick, Amanda Levete (Future Systems), Mark Dytham (Klein Dytham Architects), Nigel Coates, Tom Dixon, FAT and muf.

Pecha Kucha was founded by Klein Dytham Architects (KDA) in Tokyo in 2003. Once a month, KDA invites designers, artists, architects, students and entrepreneurs to present their designs and ideas. What sets it apart is the rapid-fire format: fourteen speakers are each asked to show twenty images and talk for twenty seconds about each one. This means the audience experiences a huge diversity of speakers in a relatively short space of time. Pecha Kucha acts as a crossroads of ideas, allowing speakers from different disciplines to talk at the same event and thus bringing together creatives who would not normally meet each other. After the presentations, it becomes a networking evening with drinks and music.

The Pecha Kucha format has spread to other cities in the world, including Berlin, Bern, Glasgow, Groningen, Los Angeles, Rotterdam, San Francisco, Stockholm and Sydney. For more information visit www.pecha-kucha.org

Above: Tom Dixon.
Right: Pecha Kucha is a dynamic forum for ideas

Location
Sadler's Wells
Rosebery Avenue
London EC1R 4TN

Pave your own way

Created and organised by Scarlet Projects with Us&Us designers
Supported by The Concrete Centre, Homestead and Marshalls

Paving slabs are a ubiquitous and boring part of our urban environment. Come along and create your own more interesting version with the help of Us &Us designers. Add bizarre aggregates to our concrete mix, or incise an image or text on to the surface. Architects, designers, children and anyone else are welcome to make their own paving stone. The best slabs will be selected later by Islington Council's Greenspace Department for laying in a local park or public space as part of the legacy of the London Architecture Biennale (any waste material will be recycled by Islington Council as hardcore).

Location
Homestead
148a St John Street
London EC1

King's Cross charette: designs on King's Cross

Organised by AJ Sponsored by Argent
Supported by London & Continental Railways

Following the news that Argent has got the go-ahead for its ambitious King's Cross Regeneration scheme, which will include around 60 architectural commissions, it has joined forces with the *Architects' Journal* to create the King's Cross Charette as part of the London Architecture Biennale. The one-day event provides an exciting opportunity for a new generation of talent to showcase their skills alongside more established practices to one of the country's most influential clients. Twenty practices are given a brief at 10am and asked to present their ideas to a panel of experts at the end of the day.

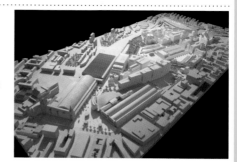

Location
The Gymnasium
Pancras Road
London NW1 2TB

Townscape sketching workshops

*Tours led by
Benedict O'Looney*

London must have once been the most drawn city in the world. However, Londoners don't seem to sketch much any more. These two afternoon workshops celebrate the architecture of the biennale route by drawing it. The sessions include demonstrations, discussions about townscape sketching techniques and a consideration of how sketching can improve our understanding of our city and its shape. All that is required is a sketchbook and a pencil: no prior skills necessary.

Above: sketch by
Benedict O'Looney,
leader of the townscape
sketching workshops

Location
Entrance of St
Bartholomew
the Great
London EC1

Run the LAB route

*Organised by
Architects
Benevolent Society*

Join the Architects Benevolent Society to run the 6km LAB route and raise funds for less fortunate members of the profession.

Starting at Myddleton Square (Angel) and finishing at Tate Modern (Southwark), the run is full of interest, passing most of the major attractions and exhibitions on the biennale route. Wind your way through London's streets, stopping to catch your breath at St Paul's Cathedral. Then, once over the Millennium Bridge, it's just a short lap round Borough Market before finishing at

Tate Modern. It's a perfect way to spend your Sunday morning as the run is gentle enough for most fitness abilities.

The Architects Benevolent Society is the only registered charity in the UK for architects, assistants, technologists and landscape architects and their dependants. It gives practical help to people of all ages that have experienced illness, accident, bereavement or other personal misfortune. We rely on your generosity to help more than 400 beneficiaries a year.

Location
Myddleton Square
London EC1

Biennale charity auction

In association with A4A and AET

A collection of personal, unusual and highly prized pieces donated by prominent UK architects and designers (including David Adjaye and Vitra) are up for auction at the most compelling charity event in architecture and design.

The Biennale Charity Auction raises money for two recently established charities that are already making a big impact in their chosen fields. This is your chance to help the UK architectural profession to strengthen its influence and impact on education and world events.

Architectural Education Trust's RIBA-AET Award assists students of architecture who encounter unexpected financial difficulties; genuine need is assessed before it is given. The charity, set up by Professor Alan Phillips, has already helped a number of talented students who may otherwise have had to abandon their studies. The award is administered by the RIBA education department. Find out more at www.riba.org.

Architects4Aid was founded by Professor Maxwell Hutchinson to raise funds, sponsor projects and train and provide architects to work on humanitarian building and shelter ventures around the world. The charity is already very active in helping to rebuild areas of Pakistan in partnership with the local community. Visit www.architectsforaid.org

Location
The Courtyard
Smithfield House
Lindsey Street
London EC1

People poem

Organised by Theresa Shiban
Supported by BDP

What's your word on architecture? Tell Building Design Partnership's writer-in-residence Theresa Shiban your favourite word relating to architecture during St Bartholomew's Fair – it could be about the design process, a material, the profession, a verb, noun or adjective, even the name of a building that inspires you – and she'll take a picture of you. The words and photographs of all participants are compiled to create the People Poem, which is displayed at BDP's office.

Location
Building Design
Partnership Piazza
Studios, The Piazza
16 Brewhouse Yard
London EC1

The Prince's Foundation extreme shopping race

Organised by The Prince's Foundation with interventions by 3run Action Team

The Prince's Foundation is hosting an Extreme Shopping Race. Thirty people armed with a shopping list in one hand and a map in the other race against the clock to locate daily essentials in two contrasting urban landscapes. The first site is structured pretty much as a traditional town would be – easy to navigate and a place where most of your daily needs are catered for. The second is a housing estate where there is nothing or very little in the way of community public space or local amenities.

With performances from the 3run Action Team, we encourage participants to use an instinctive sense of their immediate surroundings to appreciate the fast-changing face of the built environment and its effects on our everyday lives, not only socially, but also medically and culturally. One of the winning team is awarded a prize of an hour's training with a member of the 3run Action Team, worth more than £100.

The Prince's Foundation for the Built Environment is an educational charity established by the Prince of Wales to teach and demonstrate the principles of traditional urban design and architecture which put people and their communities at the centre of the design process.

Location
The Prince's
Foundation for the Built
Environment
19-22 Charlotte Road
London EC2

Speed dating of building materials

Organised by the Institute of Materials

This relaxed informal event, organised by the Institute of Materials, Minerals and Mining and sponsored by Materials KTN, involves a diverse group of experts presenting samples of innovative building materials. Visitors are given a short amount of time to examine the materials before deciding on which person they would most like to "date".

Location
The Courtyard
Smithfield House
Lindsey Street
London EC1

Left: West India Quay at Canary Wharf by HOK

The conservation book fair

Organised by SAVE
Supported by
Alan Baxter
and Associates

Featuring a range of organisations such as the Theatres Trust, SAVE Britain's Heritage and Twentieth Century Society, the conservation world gathers for its annual book fair – a chance to stock up your bookshelves with all the latest publications from the plethora of conservation organisations, as well as to catch up with friends and colleagues in the sector over a drink or two towards the end of the day.

Location
The Gallery
77 Cowcross Street
London EC1

250th anniversary Borough Market feast

Organised by
Borough Market
and Southwark
Council

A huge celebration of the Borough Market and LAB partnership. The feast is provided by traders including Peter Gott from Sillfield Farm, Mike Hill from Utobeer and a whole host of others. BBC *Master Chef* winner and author Thomasina Miers is cooking for the event, and the evening is augmented by live music.

Location
Borough Market
Borough High Street
London SE1

Party on the Green

Organised by Chetwoods in association with Clerkenwell Green Festival

Following the success of 2004's event, Chetwoods has again committed to funding the LAB party on Clerkenwell Green. With roads closed to traffic from 17.00, up to 2,000 revellers can fill up on African, Creole and Oriental treats from the food stalls dotted around the space.

Deke from The Three Kings, wearing his Evergreen Productions hat, is responsible for ensuring that an impressive selection of bands and DJs keep things moving until midnight – and he is promising a mystery guest to surpass the quality of 2004's headliners, The Blockheads.

The Three Kings and the other pubs and bars around the Green are, of course, dispensing drinks. And Chetwoods' striking kinetic structure, 'Urban Oasis', is outside The Crown, responding to the changing environment throughout the evening.

The party, open to all, is an opportunity to celebrate the events held in and around Clerkenwell Green during the London Architecture Biennale and Architecture Week. Someone once sang: "You don't have to take your clothes off to have good time, yeah, yeah!" We should have told some of the people photographed in 2004…

Location
Clerkenwell Green
London EC1

Architecture Rocks

Organised by The Architecture Foundation Supported by NME and bd

Taking its lead from great British rock acts, such as Pink Floyd, Suede and the Pet Shop Boys, that have arisen from the world of architecture, Architecture Rocks is a platform for new musical talent to be discovered. The line-up is: The Hot Shakes, Famous in Japan, Menage a Trois (Rotterdam), Horstreich (Germany) and The Farmscape Production Line. These were selected from 67 entries… who said architects don't know music?

Location
Smithfield House
Lindsey Street
London EC1

Sponsors

Organisers

Partners

Gold Sponsors

 Transport for London

 British Land

jackson|coles
construction consultants

CITY OF LONDON

LONDON
DEVELOPMENT
A G E N C Y

 Council
Southwark

 Camden

 ISLINGTON

Central London
Partnership

The Architecture Foundation

ARTS COUNCIL
ENGLAND

Silver Sponsors
Davis Langdon LLP
Savills
Cundall
Chetwoods
Price & Myers Consulting
Engineers
PRP Architects
adrem
Arup
Foster and Partners
Bissett Adams Architects
Land Securities
Building Design Partnership
Argent
London and Continental
  Railways
Akram Abu Hamdan
London Metropolitan
  University
The Concrete Centre Ltd

Bronze Sponsors
Bee Bee Developments Ltd
Great Portland Estates plc
Pipers Projects Ltd
Adams Kara Taylor
Broadgate Estates
Squire & Partners
Legal & General
London Communications
  Agency Ltd
ISG Interior Exterior
ESS
Derwent Valley Holdings plc
Kingston Smith LLP
Austin-Smith Lord LLP
The OVE ARUP Foundation
Dovetail Contract Furniture
Collyer Bristow
Fulcrum Consulting
Aedas
Skidmore, Owings &
  Merrill, Inc.
Mitsubishi Estate UK
Alford Hall Monaghan Morris
Dorrington
Lovejoy London
Susie Sainsbury
TTSP
YRM
Wilkinson Eyre Architects
Bentley
Sheppard Robson
CB Richard Ellis
Vitra
David Morley Architects
Platform for Art
Buro Happold Consulting
  Engineers

Media Partners

Architects Journal
Architectural Review
Art Review
Architecture Today
Art & Architecture Journal
Blueprint
BD
Cross Section
The Guardian
IBP
Icon
RIBA Journal

Friends
Alan Baxter & Associates
Allies & Morrison
Amin Taha
Amwell Society
Applied Information Group
Archaos
Architects Education Trust
Architects for Aid
Architectural Association
Asticus
Avanti Architects
Aylwin Communications
Barbican
Benedict O'Looney
Bennetts Associates Architects
Borough Market
Boyarsky Murphy
British Library
Camden Architects Forum
Caro Communications
College of Arms
Charles Rowan House
DSDHA
EDAW
EMS Ltd
Esterson Associates
Farmer Sharp
Fielden Clegg Bradley
Fletcher Priest Architects
Fluid
Frank Harris Estates
Giorgia Mancini
Greenhill Jenner Architects Ltd
GVA Grimley LLP
Hawkins Brown
Hines UK
HOK
Hobs Reprographics
Hopkins & Partners
Hurford Salvi Carr
Jason Bruges Studio
Jestico & Whiles
John McAslan & Partners
JWP – solutions in print ltd.
Keith Williams Architects
Knoll International Ltd
LaSalle Investment
  Management
Lloyd Baker Estate
Locum Consulting
Manhattan Loft
Materials KTN
Matteo Cainer
Measure
Merrill Lynch
More London Development Ltd
Museum of London
  Archaeology Service
New London Architecture
Peabody Estate

Piercy Connor Architects
  & Designers
PW Services
RHWL
Rolfe Judd
Sadler's Wells
The Salvation Army
Scarlet Projects
Smithfield Market
Smiths of Smithfield
Southwark Cathedral
Southwark Cyclists
spaceshift
St James' Church
St. Martin's Property Group
St. Olaf House
St Paul's Cathedral
Swanke Hayden Connell
TATE Modern
Terry Farrell & Partners
The German Gymnasium
The Globe Theatre
The Guardian Newsgroup
The Haberdashers Livery
  Company
The Photographers' Gallery
The Rookery Hotel
Tom Dyckhoff
Twentieth Century Society
Unicorn Theatre
William Bordass and
  Associates
Wordsalad
Worshipful Company of
  Butchers

LAB 250CLUB

LAB 250CLUB members

51% Studios
Adams Kara Taylor
Adjaye Associates
Adrem
Aedas
A-EM
Akera Engineers
Alan Conisbee and Associates
Alison Brooks Architects Ltd
Allford Hall Monaghan Morris
Allies and Morrison
Aram Designs Ltd
Archer Architects
Architects for Aid
Architects in Residence
architecture plb
Architecture Today
Arup
Ash Sakula Architects
Assael Architecture
Atelier Ten
Austin-Smith:Lord
Avanti Architects
Azhar Architecture
Azman Architects
BDG Work Futures
Bee Bee Developments Ltd
Bene
Benoy
Bespoke Career Management
  Ltd
Brady Mallalieu Architects
Broadway Malyan
Buckley Gray Yeoman

Burland Architects
Buro Happold
Burrell Foley Fischer
  (Architects+Urban Designers)
Buschow Henley Architects
Central London Partnership
Chapman Taylor
Chassay + Last Architects
Child Graddon Lewis Architects
  & Designers
Cities Institute
Co-Lab Architects
Complex Development
  Projects
Conran & Partners
Corporation of London
Cundall Johnston & Partners
CZWG
David Buck Landscape
  Architects Limited
David Morley Architects
Davis Langdon LLP
de Metz Forbes Knight
de Rijke Marsh Morgan Ltd
  Architects
DEGW plc
Denton Corker Marshall
Derek Mason Architects
Derwent Valley
Detail – Review of Architecture
  and Construction Details
Dewhurst MacFarlane and
  Partners
Digital Kreative
DLG Architects

Dorrington
Dovetail
dsp architecture
East City Investments
Edward Cullinan Architects
EPR Architects Limited
Eric Parry Architects
Eric R Kuhne + Associates
ESA
ARCHITECTURE:DESIGN
Faber Maunsell
Featherstone Associates
Feilden Clegg Bradley
  Architects
Fletcher Priest Architects
Foggo Associates
Foster and Partners
Fulcrum Consulting
GMW Architects
Grainger Trust plc
Greig + Stephenson
Grimshaw
Halpern
Hawkins\Brown
Hitch Mylius
HOK International Limited
Hopkins Architects
HTA Architects
Hugh Broughton Architects
Hunter Evans Architects
Hunter & Partners Ltd
Hurford Salvi Carr
Ian Ritchie Architects Ltd
Ian Simpson Architects
iGuzzini

Interface Europe Ltd
International Building Press
Jahn Lykouria Design
Jestico + Whiles
John Robertson and Associates
  Architects
John Thompson + Partners
Johnson Naylor Ltd
Kennedy O'Callaghan
  Architects
Kingston Smith
KPF
Lake Estates Ltd
Lesley Craze Gallery
Lifschutz Davidson
London Communications
  Agency
Luz Vargas Architects
m3fx
MacKay and Partners llp
Make
Manhattan Loft Corporation
Matthew Lloyd Architects LLP
Max Fordham LLP
MaxForte Media Training
McDonnell Associates Ltd
McDowell & Benedetti
Mediashore
MICE | SAMES
Michael Hadi Associates Ltd
Michael Spark Associates
Mossessian & Partners
Museum of London
  Archaeology Service (MOLAS)
Norman Disney & Young

ORMS
Peabody Trust
Penoyre + Prasad LLP
Pentagram
Peripheral Vision
Phil Coffey Architects
Piercy Conner
Pipers
Pollard Thomas Edwards
  Architects
Price & Myers
Pringle Brandon
Project Orange
PRP
Regeneration Trust
  Clerkenwell
Reid Architecture
Renton Howard Wood Levin
  LLP
Richard Rogers Parnership
Rick Mather Architects
RMJM London Ltd
S333 Architecture + Urbanism
Sadler's Wells
Shepheard Epstein Hunter
Satellite Architects
Sheppard Robson
Sidell Gibson Architects
Simon Hamilton Interior
  Design
SOM
Space Syntax
Squire and Partners
Stanhope PLC
Stanton Williams Ltd

Stiff + Trevillion Architects
stock woolstencroft
  architecture + urban
  planning
Stratton & Reekie
Swanke Hayden Connell
  Architects
Tamesis
Techniker
Terry Farrell & Partners
The Concrete Centre
The Manser Practice
The Prince's Foundation
The Zetter Restaurant &
  Rooms
thomas.matthews
tp bennet architects
Thompson Hamilton Design
  Consultants
Transport Planning Initiatives
Trehearne Architects
ttsp
Universal Design Studio
Verve Properties Ltd
Vic Naylor Restaurant and Bar
Walters + Cohen
Weston Williamson
Wolff Olins
Working Visions Limited
YRM
Zumbtobel Staff Lighting

Photographers credits

Covers: Getty; Mirjam von Arx; Guildhall Library, City of London
p.6: M3fx
p.8 Phil Sayer
p.10: Peter Jordon/PA/Empics
p.12: Getty; Corbis
p13: Burstein Collection/Corbis
p.14: Stapleton Collection/Corbis;
p.15: Museum of Transport
p.16-17: Getty
p.18: Howard Davies/Corbis
p.19: Fine Art Photographic Library/Corbis
p.20: Museum of London /HIP/TopFoto.co.uk
p.20-23: LAB
p.24: Hulton-Deutsch Collection/CORBIS
p.25: Jason Bruges Studio
p.26: Country Life
p.30-31: AIG London
p.32-35: Jason Bruges Studio; Greig & Stephenson
p.36-37: Benedict O'Looney
p.38-41: View Pictures; Nick Guttridge; Foster and Partners
p.42-43: Piercy Conner
p.44-45: New Design Research Studio
p.46-51: Nick Robertson; Wordsalad; Foster and Partners; Bisset Adams
p.52-55: Miller Hare Associates
p.56-57: Roderick Coyne; Modern House Estate
p.58-59: TFL Visual Image Services
p.60: Fabrice Bourrelly
p.61: Minnie Weisz
p.62: Peter Saville; Scarlet Projects
p.63: Nina Noor; Andrew Stiff
p.64-65: leit-werk
p.66-69: Phil Sayer; Agora Photos
p.70: Lesley Craze Gallery
p.71: Munkenbeck + Marshall
p.72-73: Fast
p.74-75: Nicholas Kane
p.76-77: Ian Fussell Price & Myers

p.78: Mike Franks
p.79: Michael Kantor
p.80-81: David Morley Architects
p.82-83: Lynch Architects
p.84: Farrells
p.85: Yanki Lee; exhibit
p.86-87: RHWL Architects
p.88-89: Jaime Gilli
p.90-91:Elly Tabberer, Architects in Residence
p.92: Peter Newton
p.93: ORMS
p.94: Graeme Evans
p.95: Helen Bendon
p.96-97: London Metropolitan University; Central St Martin's; University of Westminster; Robert Gordon University
p.98-99: Chetwoods
p.100-101: Caravajal and Davey
p.102: David Carr-Smith
p.103-105: Alan Williams
p.106-107: Adrian Scrivner
p.108-109: Alison Dring; Elegant Embellishments
p.110: Feilden Clegg Bradley
p.111: Aitken Leclercq Ltd
p.112-113: Stefano Goldberg; Hayes Davids and John Maclean
p.114-115: Sanne Pepper; Inigo Bujedo Aguirre Photography Ltd; Charlie Koolhaas; Jeff Kaufman
p.116-118: Penguin's Press Site; Dan Chung; The Guardian; Alex Macnaughton; Boris Johnson MP's Office; Courtesty Janet Street Porter
p.119: Nick Robertson; Wordsalad
p.120: Kumiko Shimizu
p.121: BBC London
p.122: Ken Sharp; RIBA journal; Jeremy Hunt; Blueprint
p.124: Architecture for Humanity
p.125: Farrell & Partners
p.126: Collection Richard Wentworth
p.127: London Borough of Camden
p.128: Southwark Council;

Allied London
p.129: Marcus Wilcocks; DA Research Centre UAL
p.130: Tate
p.132-133: Planet Photo
p.134-135: Nik Milner; John Tramper
p.136: King's Cross Voices
p.137-139: PTEa
p.140: Richard Bryant
p.141: Greig + Stephenson
p.142: Mike Franks
p.143: Jos Boys
p.144: Culture Heritage Resources
p.145: Will Laslett
p.146-147: Hélène Binet; Keith Williams Architects
p.148: RHWL; Courtesy of Space Syntax
p.149: Greig + Stephenson
p.150-153: Courtesy Mirjam von Arx
p.154: Tom Heneghan; ©AA Photo & Film Library; 51% Studios; Emily Richardson
p.155: Architecture Association
p.156: London & Continental Railways
p.157: Paul Kelly
p.158: Courtesy Farmer Sharp
p.160-161: Wilkinson Eyre Architects
p.162-163: Sinisa Rodic; 51% studios
p.164: Courtesy Morven Mitchell, Price & Myers
p.165: Catharine Kidd
p.166: Courtesy the artist Christian Sievers
p.168 : Courtesy Claire Ireland
p.169: Icon magazine
p.170: Architects' Journal
p.171: Benedict O'Looney
p.172: Theresa Shiban
p.173: Outokumpu's Hyclad
p.174: Greig + Stephenson
p.175: Chetwoods; James Branch